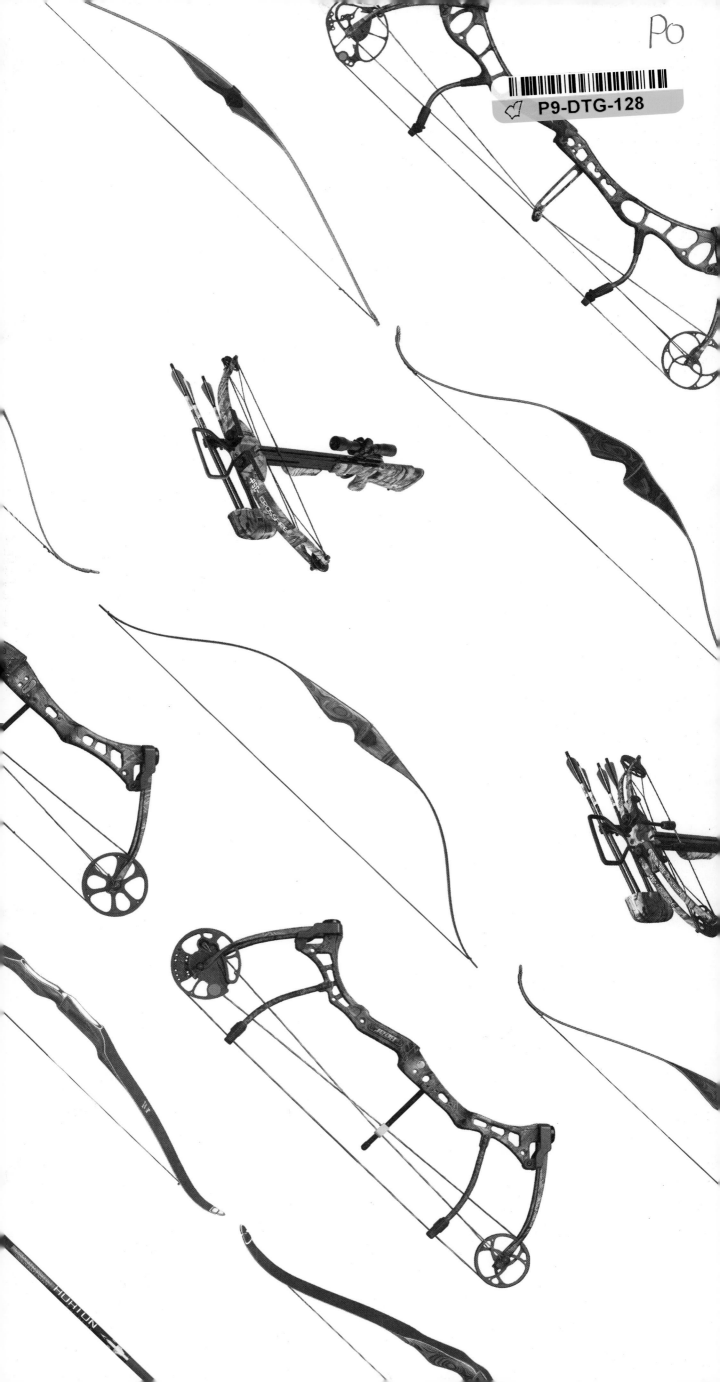

ARCHERY

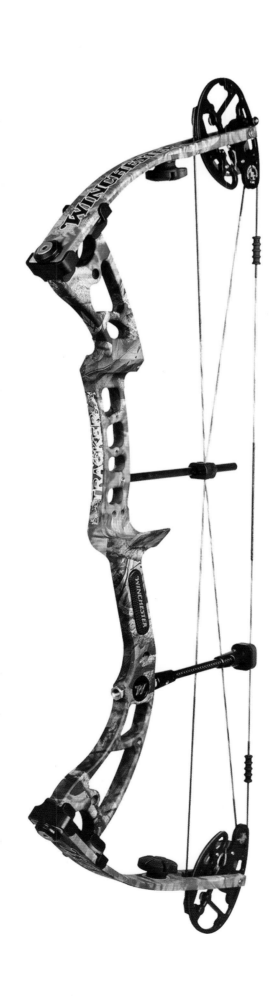

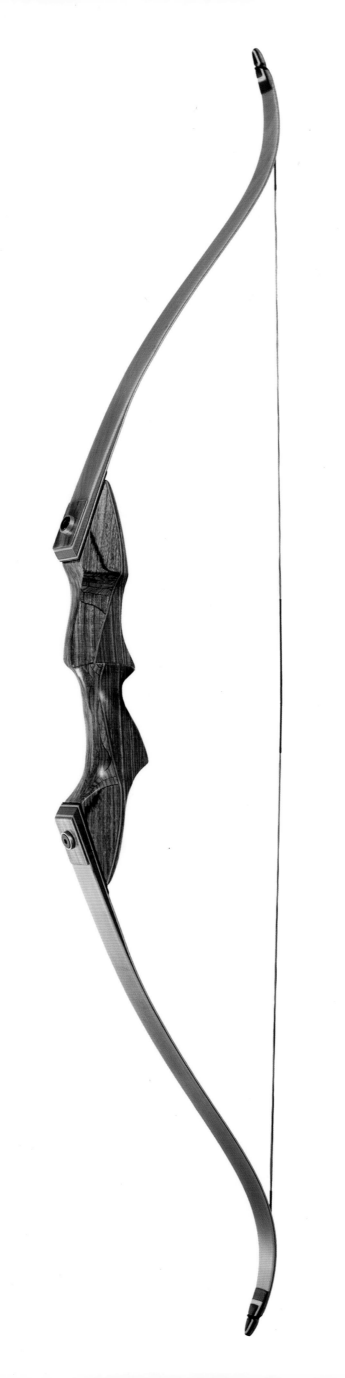

ARCHERY

Rick Sapp

3 1336 09526 0270

THUNDER BAY
P·R·E·S·S

San Diego, California

Thunder Bay Press
An imprint of the Baker & Taylor Publishing Group
10350 Barnes Canyon Road, San Diego, CA 92121
www.thunderbaybooks.com

First Published 2012

Produced by TAJ Books International LLC
113E Melbourne Park Circle
Charlottesville, Virginia
22901

www.tajbooks.com

Copyright ©2012 Taj Books International LLC

All notations of errors or omissions should be addressed to Thunder Bay Press, Editorial Department, at the
above address. All other correspondence (author inquiries, permissions) concerning the content of this book
should be addressed to TAJ Books, 113E Melbourne Park Circle, Charlottesville, Virginia 22901, info@tajbooks.com.

ISBN-13: 978-1-60710-637-1
ISBN-10: 1-60710-637-X

Library of Congress Cataloging-in-Publication Data

Sapp, Rick.
  Archery / Rick Sapp.
    p. cm.
  Includes index.
  ISBN 978-1-60710-637-1
  1. Archery. 2. Bowhunting. 3. Bow and arrow. I. Title.
  GV1185.S23 2012
  799.3'2--dc23
  2012021884

Printed in China.

1 2 3 4 5 16 15 14 13 12

CONTENTS

Introduction

The bow and arrow did not make their way to the continent of Australia until recent times. Australian aborigines shared a very simple but effective tool complex. Here they sharpen and haft stone axes. Some sites bear traces of deep grooves in the rock surfaces and were obviously convenient spots for grinding ax edges into shape for thousands of years.

It is impossible to state with certainty when the bow and arrow first appeared. The archery tool complex— bow, string, arrow, fletching, and arrowhead—may have evolved in several areas independently over time. It's safe to say that men used bows and arrows 20,000 years ago. Some researchers claim the archaeological record can trace its use as far back as 65,000 years ago.

Ancient archery artifacts are found in caves and graves on every continent except Antarctica. Surviving art and religious fragments also offer tantalizing images of its ancestry.

What is certainly true is that men and women were just as keen to solve the problems of survival then as now. When people lived off the land, procuring one's daily sustenance was a challenge. Another was to keep the upper hand in the hunter–prey relationship.

The tools one is born with are all essential for survival in a world where food is hand-to-mouth. Grabbing and gobbling sufficed for our australopithecine ancestors, for our Neanderthal and Cro-Magnon relatives, and even for today's baboons and chimpanzees, both of which species are stronger, faster, and more ferocious than humans, and in some cases, just as tactically intelligent. Surviving in a world where one was born naked and hairless, however, was at best difficult. Life was short and hard.

The atlatl tool (or woomera in Australia) surely came first. The atlatl, or spear thrower, is an extension of the arm, a longer lever that allows a spear to travel a greater distance at greater speed and hit with significantly greater force than is possible with the unaided arm. Atlatls allowed hunters to distance themselves from game and throw a heavy spear at the speed of a major league fastball, perhaps 100 mph.

How man made the leap to the bow is a mystery. The first bow might have been a musical instrument, a child's toy, or a utilitarian gadget like a fire drill. Nevertheless, someone recognized its possibilities and the primitive bow and arrow spread to every inhabited continent. Whereas a man could carry one or perhaps two spears and an atlatl, an archer could carry a bow and a dozen or more arrows in a quiver.

There were trade-offs, of course, in force, distance, and penetration. Men still carried spears, of course. At first the tips were dried and fire-hardened, but soon they were tipped with sharp flint heads and ultimately with iron. The men of prehistory also developed the deadly sling, which worked on the same principle as

Bhimbetka rock painting showing a man riding on a horse and men with various instruments including bows and arrows. The Bhimbetka rock shelters are an archaeological World Heritage site located in the Indian state of Madhya Pradesh.

An Australian aborigine holding a spear thrower, or woomera, with which he increases his throwing power. The woomera appeared on the continent about 5,000 years ago. The bow and arrow is first recorded as appearing in Australia in the mid-nineteenth century.

the atlatl, but with an effective distance of hundreds of yard—more than twice the distance an atlatl could be thrown.

Harnessing the Power of the Gods

The bow and arrow used not only a man's strength, but also harnessed the power of nature, and that brought the gods into play. Apollo shot arrows infected with the plague into the Greek encampment during the Trojan War. Later, he guided Paris's deadly arrow to the heel of Greek super-hero Achilles.

Along with the Mycenaean Greeks and Trojans, almost every ancient culture celebrated the advantages conveyed by the bow and arrow and associated the compound tool with their gods.

The warrior goddess Satet protected the pharaoh and the southern borders of ancient Egypt. In her dual role as goddess of fertility she brought the annual Nile River floods and purified the deceased with water from the underworld (the mythical source of the Nile).

Rama, the seventh avatar of Vishnu in Hinduism, shot an undying arrow across all time and the universe. According to mythology, the day it falls to earth will bring the end of the world or perhaps the end of all evil on earth, and thus uphold dharma and righteousness.

On the Great Plains of North America, the Blackfoot Indian creation myth tells how Old Man (Napi) was walking north and creating as he went. He created bighorn sheep and buffalo. Then he molded people from clay, but the first people were poor and naked; they did not know how to do anything for themselves. So Old Man taught them to make bows and arrows, and how to hunt the animals for food.

Whatever the origin or relation of the tools to the supernatural, men immediately began to refine their bows and arrows. They discovered the best raw materials and techniques for shaping bows and straightening arrows: some woods, particularly yew, were more suited to the stress of simultaneous stretching and compression than others. They discovered that a hardened arrowhead would penetrate the skin of

A hunting scene painted on the walls of a cave in the Tassili n'Ajjer mountain range in southeast Algeria. More than 15,000 petroglyphs have been identified in caves, many showing hunting with spears and bows and arrow.

animals, and they learned to shape sharp heads from rocks and then fasten them to arrows with the greased intestinal strings of animals. They discovered that bird feathers affixed to the opposite end of an arrow stabilized its flight and provided greater accuracy. They embarked on a process which to this very day has not ended.

Fun and Games and Weapons

The bow and arrow were effective weapons in human conflicts. Long before the refinement of gunpowder to fire a lethal projectile, bows and arrows were used by armies as well as by individual assassins.

Prior to the modern era, classical civilizations—Mongols, Parthians, Assyrians, Persians, Koreans, Japanese—fielded immense armies of archers. Mounted warriors raced across the fields firing as their horses ran. Their iron-tipped arrows were deadly at hundreds of yards and especially destructive to other masses of lightly armored infantry.

Wherever elephants lived—in Southeast Asia, India, and Africa—archers rode them into battle. The combination of an immense, armored beast maddened by the confused pricks of spears or arrows and of carrying partially protected archers was as effective

At the Convention of World Mongolians, July 2010, in Ulan-Ude, Buryatia, Russia, an unidentified archer participates in a Mongolian archery competition.

Introduction

The original illustration by French artist Jacques le Monye de Morgues (1533–1588) was made based on his visit to Florida in 1564 as a member of Jean Ribault's ill-fated expedition to the New World.

Arrow slits were typical features of medieval castles such as Corfe Castle in Dorset, England. An archer would have stood here to shoot from the well-protected position with a wide field of view and field of fire. The thin vertical aperture allowed archers to vary the elevation and direction of a bowshot but made it difficult for attackers to return fire accurately, since there is only a small target at which to aim. The invention of the arrowslit is attributed to Greek mathematician and physicist Archimedes during the Siege of Syracuse, 214–212 BC.

A flaked stone arrowhead could be made as sharp as a modern knife. This arrowhead represents the Dalton Culture about 8,000 BC. Dalton was a tool complex and mixed farming/hunter-gatherer lifestyle that emerged across the mid-south of the U.S. at the end of the Paleo-Indian period.

against infantry as are modern battle tanks. Alexander the Great faced them, and Hannibal marched them over the Alps and down into Italy.

The mechanical ingenuity of bow makers (called bowyers) developed radically over thousands of years of use. A peak of the art combined mounted warriors with recurved composite bows. These short, powerful bows were wielded with devastating effectiveness by Mongol cavalry who could rain death down on opponents from a quarter-mile away. These were no simple stick-and-string bows. Beginning with a core of wood, Mongol bowyers faced the stave with horn and backed it with sinew, thus allowing for tremendous compression on the horn side and stretching on the sinew side. This composition was bound together with animal glue and its effectiveness carried Genghis Khan from the steppes of Mongolia to the Danube River, a kingdom larger than the United States.

The bow and arrow were also effective in the hands of individual ninjas and assassins. Nearly 5,300 years ago a tattooed, 45-year-old man climbed into the Alps along what is today the Austrian-Italian border. He wore warm fur garments and carried a bow and fourteen arrows, a sharp flint knife, and a valuable copper ax. At some point, "Oetzi, the Iceman" was shot in the back with a flint-tipped arrow and his skull was bashed in with a rock. Hikers discovered his ice-entombed, mummified remains in 1991.

The incident that most famously demonstrates the effect of a single arrow dates to October 14, 1066. That afternoon, according to legend, King Harold Godwinson was struck in the eye by an arrow. When Harold collapsed in pain at Hastings, English resistance also collapsed and William the Conqueror's army of bowmen, cavalry, and infantry swept toward London to crown him William I.

The great age of the bow and arrow was doomed, of course, as chemists and alchemists around the globe experimented with the magic of explosive powders.

Still, the bow provided romance and legend, even if the dates and indeed the actual events associated with their use cannot always be verified.

For example, under the Roman Catholic Pope Innocent II, the Second Lateran Council banned the use of crossbows in 1139, but only against Christians. In the 1260s, during competition before the sheriff of Nottingham, Robin Hood shot arrows so accurately that they split other arrow shafts down the center in the very heart of the targets. And William Tell shot an apple off his son's head in Switzerland in 1307, stoking the Swiss fever for independence.

During the era of Crécy (1346) and Poitiers (1356), a small army, principally of English longbowmen, obliterated the flower of French knighthood. The French knights ultimately took revenge, however, at the battle of Patay in 1429. These archers drew bows with—by today's standards—astonishing draw weights of up to 200 pounds and could be permanently disfigured from the extreme effort. It is not surprising that conventional armor was no defense against the iron arrow heads.

All of these tales emanated from the age of minstrels when stories passed by word of mouth and people longed for heroes. This romantic period literally ended with a bang.

The End…in a Flash!

Men used ignitable gunpowder formulations a thousand years ago, although the powders were generally suitable only for fireworks and magic tricks. In the Medieval Era, these formulations made their way along trade routes from China (and as part of Mongol conquests in the thirteenth century) to the Middle East and subsequently to Europe. In all of these regions, men experimented with saltpeter and found that it could be used to propel iron balls with terrifying, body-splintering results. Indeed, firearms may have been present at the battle of Crécy in 1346, arguably the pinnacle of archery supremacy. At that moment, the bow and arrow were served notice that their favored status as a weapon for warfare and hunting was doomed.

As firearms grew in importance and sophistication over the course of half a millennium, archery declined. With it went the lance and pike, the ax and mace, the sword and spear and dagger, all gradually replaced by hand cannons and flintlocks. And yet, little ever completely disappears.

In the early days of the second millennium, a skilled archer could accurately shoot a dozen arrows in the space of one musket shot because the reloading process of early guns was especially tedious. As a consequence, the bow and arrow did not immediately disappear from the battlefields or hunting grounds. In North America, Indians famously hunted buffalo with the bow and arrow, both on foot and from horseback, into the late nineteenth century. The American archer, inventor, and manufacturer Fred Bear bought a diminutive bow from a Central African pygmy hunter in the 1960s. As late as 2008, tribesmen in the Amazon jungles were filmed attempting to bring down an airplane with bows and arrows.

Eventually, however, faced by the development of repeating firearms, smokeless powders, and self-contained cartridges, the bow and arrow almost disappeared from civilized consciousness. Firearms were simply more effective for warfare or hunting at

The bow and arrow have often changed the course of history. In October 1066, William the Conqueror invaded England from Normandy. Fresh from a victory against invading Vikings, England's last Anglo-Saxon king, Harold Godwinson, marched his exhausted army hundreds of miles to meet the new threat. The English shield wall held fast until Harold was apparently hit in the eye with a steel-tipped arrow. Seeing their leader terribly wounded, the English broke and fled. The Bayou Tapestry records that battle and Harold is seen (arguably) with an arrow in his face and subsequently being killed by a mounted Norman knight. Credit: From the Bayeux Tapestry, created about 1070, thought to be commissioned by Matilda of Flanders, Odo of Bayeux, or Edith of Wessex.

A 2012 historical reenactment of the April 1242 Battle of Lake Peipus between the Republic of Novgorod and the Livonian branch of the Teutonic knights.

Introduction

The native Rikbaktsa peoples are hunters, gatherers, and agriculturalists who live in the Amazon rain forest of northwest Mato Grosso Province, Brazil. Traditionally, male children receive their first bow between the ages of three and five years old. In the photo, a Rikbaktsa archer competes in Brazil's 2007 Indigenous Games.

any distance.

Yet the bow and arrow tradition persisted. In Japan, even as the emperor outlawed samurai, archery merged into a meditative corner of Zen Buddhism. On the steppes of Asia and as far west as Hungary, descendants of Mongol cavalry continued to practice the skills of their ancestors. Today, public archery is often part of a festival-driven competition such as the Mongolian *Naadam*, or "three games of men," with the other two games being wrestling and horse racing.

In Europe, a more formal archery was eventually incorporated into the modern Olympic Games in Paris in 1900. Eight years later at the London games, women were allowed to participate. Yet, differences existed among national archery teams with some emphasizing shooting from horseback, while others preferred the crossbow. Some national archery teams still excluded women, and the shooting form of archery strayed as far as the variously spelled "popinjay," which tied birds, originally live parrots or pigeons, and later only tufts of feathers, to tall poles for target practice.

Even for the nascent and argumentative Olympic rules committees this situation was too disorganized. The lack of uniform international rules caused archery to be dropped from the Olympic program after 1920. It was not included again until the ill-fated 1972 games in Munich.

Archery remained a sports stepchild until 1931 when the International Archery Federation, or Federation International de Tir a l'Arc (FITA), was founded in Poland by a committee of seven countries: France, Czech Republic, Sweden, Poland, United States, Hungary, and Italy. Today, FITA is composed of nearly 150 member associations representing the world's nation-states. Its purpose focuses on the Olympics and on conducting archery events that conform to stylized, static Olympic rules and principles.

The 1972 Olympic Games in Munich, which were the games interrupted by terrorist attacks on Israeli athletes, were the proving ground for FITA's rules. Competitors shot 36 arrows for a single competition and 72 arrows for a double. Men shot from 90, 70, 50, and 30 meters, whereas women shot from 70, 60, 50, and 30 meters. In the 1988 Olympic games in Seoul, Korea, team competition was added. Today, four archery events make up the Olympic program: men's and women's individual and team competitions.

Archery has reinvented itself in the twentieth century. Modern archery has assumed two main forms: Olympic-style competition and hunting with the bow and arrow. Other, less publicized archery events do, however, persist around the world: contests from horseback, popinjay, archery golf, kyudo, and 3D.

Ishi and Modern Bowhunting

Millions of archers hunt recreationally with the bow, primarily in economically prosperous countries such as the United States, Canada, and to a lesser extent,

Mongolian Naadam archery

14

A 2005 replica of a Roman ballista called a scorpio and reenactors firing one. The standard was 60 scorpios per legion or one for each of the 60 centuriae composing the legion. A centuria was originally composed of 100 men, but with the Marian reforms in the late second century BC was lowered to 60–80 men.

Continental Europe, or they venture to find exotic game in less prosperous countries such as Namibia or Uzbekistan. The rise of modern archery hunting or bowhunting began in the nineteenth century, principally in the United States where widespread admiration of the Native American way of life coexisted with the competing lust to exterminate Indian tribes and seize their land and its resources.

In 1911, the sole surviving member of the Yahi tribe, a middle-aged man called Ishi, fled starving from the isolation of the northern California forest. He was eventually given refuge by anthropologists at the University of California-Berkeley where he lived five years as both a specimen for study and as a research assistant. Prior to his death from tuberculosis, Ishi taught many people to enjoy native crafts, among them building and shooting the bow and arrow, through his relationship with the Museum of Anthropology in San Francisco. One of the people Ishi first befriended was his doctor, Saxton Pope. As a child and young adult, Dr. Pope had experimented with bows and arrows. His friendship with Ishi reignited his interest in archery.

As word of Ishi's existence spread, Will Compton, an experienced bowyer who had learned his archery skills at a young age from Sioux Indians in Nebraska, traveled from Oregon to California to meet Ishi. In 1915, while at the Panama-Pacific Exposition in San Franciso, Compton met a young outdoorsman and hunter named Art Young. Compton introduced Young to Dr. Pope and Ishi. The four became fast friends, building bows and arrows and hunting together. Eventually Pope and Young hunted grizzly bear and African lions, traveling to Greenland and Alaska. Young also lectured to popularize the sport and one of the young men he energized in Michigan was Fred Bear, who founded Bear Archery in 1939.

Today there are three million licensed bowhunters in North America, all of whom owe the existence of their hobby to Ishi. Furthermore, wildlife departments recognize the bow and arrow as sufficient for taking any big game animal, from whitetail deer to musk ox. Indeed, thousands of American and international archers travel the world to hunt: to Florida for alligator, to Tanzania for lion, to Australia for water buffalo, to Alaska for moose, and to Russia for brown bears.

The basic instrument of archers around the world is the traditionally styled recurve bow, which varies

In this detail of a painting from Germany dated to around 1475, crossbowmen are taking part in the martyrdom of St. Sebastian.

Introduction

Ishi taught Saxton Pope and Art Young to build and shoot bows and arrows the Indian way and is thus considered by many to be the patron saint of bowhunting in America. Left, with his bow and arrow; right, his quiver full of arrows.

from region to region. But man is an inquisitive and inventive tool-making animal, so he maintains traditions such as archery, even though they are not especially practical, and continues to innovate, adding new methods, new materials, and new instruments to his repertoire. Archery has always been a craft that rewarded innovation, even after its original benefits as a survival-tool complex became antiquated. Now startling new instruments are finding their way into hunting camps and competition venues across the world, taking over old styles and inventing new.

Bows of the World

Three distinct types of bows are shot around the world. The stick bow, or basic longbow, has a brilliant heritage, dating thousands of years before the recurves of mounted Mongol warriors or the longbow wielded by English yeomen. Early crossbows, essentially a horizontal bow mounted on a gun stock, appeared in Asia in about 1,000 BC. The compound, or wheeled, bow was effectively invented in the middle of the twentieth century.

Longbows and Recurves

The longbow as a single shaped piece of wood is today referred to as a self-bow (or perhaps flat-bow), and it was surely the first purposefully constructed bow: dried, shaped, greased, and sanded, then notched to hold a string. Equipped with a string of dried, greased animal intestines, it performed well with wooden arrows and either a tiny knapped flint or a bone arrowhead. The cross-sectional shape of the flat bow resembled a rectangle.

A step-up in power and resiliency was the longbow, whose cross-section required a "D" shape with relatively narrow limbs. Bow lengths of approximately a shooter's height gave the archer a long, but manageable draw and made the most of the energy that the bow could store. It is not difficult to imagine thousands of years of experimentation with the tools and raw materials available in prehistory: wood, bone, and stone. When drawn, the longbow

describes a sweet and uninterrupted arc.

Longbows may be built from various woods, including Osage orange and mulberry, even bamboo, lemonwood, pine, or hickory, but the qualities of yew attracted early bowyers. Sectioning a yew to make bows requires careful attention to the layering of the bole, because the heartwood has excellent compressive characteristics, whereas the outer sapwood is good in tension.

The strength of the longbow was that a bowyer could build several per day. Unfortunately, it had three weaknesses. One, it was especially vulnerable to splitting at the narrow tip, which had to be notched to hold the string on the bow's centerline. This was eventually remedied by gluing notched horn to the tip and placing the string in the notch of the horn. Two, the longbow was, as its name implies, long, and although it was entirely adequate for foot soldiers or hunting, it could not be shot effectively from horseback. Three, the longbow required extensive training before the bowyer became proficient and continued training was necessary. According to legend, French soldiers threatened to cut off two fingers of the right hand of any English archer whom they captured.

Today, the longbow has returned to fashion, even though the typical launched arrow is less than 180 feet per second. Its popularity in a small sub-group could be a reaction to the pervasive commercial culture—or perhaps because of it. Bowyers skilled in longbow production have proliferated to the point that excellent trees and hence wood staves—the raw, unworked wooden staffs from which the bow is constructed—are increasingly rare. It is thought that good yew for English longbows was already becoming rare in the sixteenth century!

Bowyers who are building longbows are crafting beautiful and eminently functional bows. Modern longbows are often laminated with dyed wood and fiberglass or built in a takedown model with a metal hinge. A takedown version allows the bow to be folded in the middle and makes shipping and storage easy.

Longbow strings may still be built in the traditional

The battle of Crécy: Edward the Black Prince (1330–1376), son of Edward III of England, commanding the English army including longbow archers against the strong French troops. In this battle a much smaller English army, commanded by Edward III of England and heavily outnumbered by Philip VI of France's force, was victorious as a result of superior weaponry and tactics. It was a battle where the effectiveness of the English longbow, used en masse, was proven against armored knights. Credit: From the fifteenth-century illuminated manuscript Chronicles by Jean Froissart.

A fourteenth-century archery reenactment

Introduction

In this 300-year-old depiction of the ten-armed Hindu goddess Durga, she is mounted on a tiger to fight the buffalo-demon Mahishasura. Watching in the clouds above are celestial beings called Devas. Durga has armed herself with swords, spears, rope, and a shield, as well as a bell, a conch-shell trumpet, and apparently an incense burner. She has shot Mahishasura twice in the head with her arrows and is pictured with a drawn bow preparing to shoot the demon again.

Flemish twist manner, but the materials now are most likely a petrochemical-based synthetic, such as DynaFlight 97 or B50 Dacron.

The modern recurve stickbow is a takedown with a metal handle. This means the limbs are built separately from the handle and are often different materials entirely. They fasten to the handle with bolts, which trims the size of a shipping or storage container from about 50 to 30 inches. Single-piece and takedown models are commercially available and aluminum or hard plastic shipping containers are available for both.

Stick bows are made commercially by large manufacturers and thousands of individual craftsmen around the world. Bowyers often use exotic wood, such as rosewood, Bubinga, Shedua, and "hard rock" maple, as laminates for handles (called risers). Limbs are made of exquisitely layered fiberglass and maple. Larger manufacturers build both single-piece wood and takedown models. Within the last fifty years, companies have built metal handles. The standard now is a takedown handle machined from a solid block of aluminum. The limbs of the bow are usually laminated sheets of maple and fiberglass; the latter is often referred to as "carbon" in industry and consumer publications.

Unlike the fashion with current compound bows, the string of a stick bow—longbow or recurve—is drawn, held, and released with the fingers. Of course, the fingers are usually protected from the bite of the string by a leather glove or multilayer tab.

In 1964, while hunting from Camp Ruark on the Save River in Mozambique, Fred Bear became one of the few modern bowhunters to take an elephant with a bow and arrow. His guides were Wally Johnson, Jr., (left) and Amadeu Peixe (middle) called "Fish." Bear was shooting a laminated recurve bow with a four-blade Razorhead mounted on a heavy arrow. Bear gave the arrow extra weight for better penetration by inserting an aluminum arrow shaft inside a shaft of fiberglass.

The Crossbow

The crossbow has a more convoluted history than the vertical bow. In modern design it is built with new materials, and though it would certainly be recognizable by Asian archers of two or three thousand years ago, it has basically acquired an almost entirely new appearance.

In its early form, the crossbow promised the delivery of a deadly missile even when shot by unskilled hands. The Chinese even invented repeating crossbows as well as crossbows that shot multiple arrows at once. Greek and Roman armies had huge crossbows, some even chariot-mounted as ballistas, and very small crossbows known as scorpios, which were considered sniper weapons.

Crossbowman executing Saint Sebastian. Detail of a figure from the Upper Rhine, around 1480 in linden wood. Credit: Bayerisches Nationalmuseum, München, Germany.

The English yew longbow measured about six feet long and was used for hunting and warfare. It was a dominant weapon between 1250 and 1450. It was particularly effective against the French during the Hundred Years' War at the battles of Crécy (1346), Poitiers (1356), and Agincourt (1415). Identical bows were used across northern and western Europe and many yew bowstaves were imported from Spain from the fourteenth century onward. The earliest longbow known from England, found at Ashcott Heath, Somerset, is dated to 2665 BC.

The longer, vertical bows required a lifetime of familiarity, certainly in prehistoric cultures when a man was at the same time a skilled craftsman and a hunter. The benefit of the crossbow was that armies of slaves or peasants could bring formidable firepower to combat. Tipped with an iron head, a crossbow arrow, especially when shot by massed formations of archers, could overwhelm armored cavalry.

The benefits of the crossbow—a heavy killing bolt and a short learning curve—were counterbalanced by problems. Compared to the English longbow, for instance, the Genoese crossbowmen employed by the French at Crécy experienced a number of difficulties. The range of their bulky crossbow was shorter and the time between shots was longer; the longbowmen could execute an effective shot about every five seconds— about five times faster than a skilled crossbowman.

Two additional difficulties presented at that battle. A sudden thunderstorm prior to the battle wet the crossbow strings, slackening them, and decreasing their range and power. Strings of the era were strong fibers selected from materials that would not fray: whipcord, linen, hemp, twisted mulberry root, and sinew. So unlike the longbow, the crossbow could not easily or quickly be unstrung. The other problem was the recocking effort, which required the Genoese to crouch behind shields as they prepared again to shoot, but unfortunately the Genoese neglected to bring shields to the field of battle.

A final obstacle for the French in this 1346 battle were the Genoese themselves. The mounted Frenchmen were nobility, and it was frustrating for them to require the services of commoners. But when the Genoese found they could not match the English archers, they withdrew. This so angered the Frenchmen that they killed numbers of the Genoese archers as the French noblemen charged past them and toward the English lines.

Early crossbows were heavy, bulky, and unwieldy. Draw weights could range to several thousand pounds as enormous, wheel-mounted ballistas fired bolts of enormous size at enemy fortifications or troop formations. Individual crossbowmen cocked the bow with a winch or lever, and although they were deadly, they were also slow, subject to weather conditions, and, in unskilled hands, relatively inaccurate.

Today's crossbow is essentially a very short bow that can be shot in the manner of a gun. It is shoulder fired and released with a trigger. The bow mounts to, and is held horizontally on, the fore-end of a stock. The synthetic bowstring is drawn back toward the shooter into the trigger housing where the safety engages it. A crossbow shoots short arrows, often referred to as bolts, that kill by causing hemorrhage.

Despite occasional secret experimentation, the era of the crossbow as a military weapon is long past. Today

According to legend, William Tell was a strong man and an expert shot with the crossbow. In 1307 he refused to bow before the hat of Gessler, the Austrian overlord, and was forced to shoot an apple off his son's head. Tell later assassinated the cruel Austrian and sparked the rebellion which led to Swiss independence. The bronze statue of Tell shows the Swiss national hero with his crossbow and accompanied by his son, Walter. Erected in 1895, the monument stands in Altdorf, Switzerland. It was sculpted by Richard Kissling.

Modern-day crossbow

An unidentified Hungarian rider demonstrates archery on horseback at the yearly organized "Maltezer camp" in Valcele, Romania.

it is strictly a hunting tool, but is also used in some minor competitive events. It can be mastered more quickly than the vertical bow. It can be shot from a rest position, like a gun, and its arrows tend to be faster with a slightly greater range and a flatter trajectory than a vertical bow. It does not require continual attention to tuning and is not as temperamental as a high-speed vertical bow. Riflemen are immediately comfortable with it. Older bowhunters also find that if a crossbow is equipped with a cocking aid, it does not tax their shoulders as much as a fast compound bow.

Today's crossbows are built with wheels (compound) and without wheels (recurve) at the end of the limbs. Proponents argue vehemently for the benefits of each, but with care each style performs capably in the field. The speed of their arrows depends on draw weight and length of pull. Crossbows require little maintenance, can be equipped with a scope and sling, and are tooled to accept a quiver with arrows.

Much work has recently been done in two areas of crossbow performance: cocking and silencing. Not long ago, crossbows were exceptionally noisy. Thus, in a hunting situation, they were a one-shot weapon because if a game animal was not hit it would become so alarmed that it would run away before the bow could be recocked and reloaded, all of which requires a great deal of effort and movement. Now, numerous silencing devices can be attached to the string and to the limbs to dampen the noise of a shot.

The second development has been in building cocking devices. A heavy, 150-pound draw-weight crossbow must be cocked, that is, the string drawn from the forward position to the safety latch, very carefully in order to ensure that the string is centered in the stock. To cock a normal crossbow, the bowyer puts a foot in the stirrup, bends over and manually draws the string back, one hand on either side, into the receiver. To make this less arduous, manufacturers have developed a variety of cranks and rope devices that make cocking easier on the back.

Commercial crossbows have terrific shooting characteristics in the hands of the average archer.

They are easy to shoot, weigh about the same as a rifle (seven to eight pounds, fully loaded), have a normal range of 40 to 60 yards, and speeds—at the high end—upward of 400 fps.

Wood is no longer the building material for crossbow stocks and bolts. Wooden units were heavy and tended to swell with absorbed moisture. The new materials are lightweight carbon-impregnated fiberglass stocks and limbs with machined aluminum prods and synthetic strings; catgut has long been out of style. The new crossbow is built with a rail for a scope, either a low fixed-power or red-dot scope is preferred because of the arrow's relatively limited range. Arrows are either specially constructed aluminum or carbon fiberglass tubes. The front end is tipped with a broadhead that may weigh as much as 150 grains, or about one-third of an ounce.

The Compound Bow

The most recent incarnation of the bow and arrow is the compound, or cam, bow. Unlike classic stick bows, powerful recurve bows, or the crossbow, the history of the compound bow is precisely dated. A compound bow is a fancy lever using cables and pulleys in the shape of eccentrics to bend the bow limbs. Because compound limbs are exceptionally stiff, they store more energy than recurves or longbows. Thus, when the archer draws the bow string, which is attached to the pulley, the pulley rotates and the archer is able to gain a mechanical advantage over the stiff and now-bending limbs.

Thus, all other things being equal, in well-tuned systems a great deal more energy is stored in compound bows in comparison to the amount stored in stick bows. More energy typically means the bowyer can shoot a faster arrow a greater distance with increased energy delivery. This results in flatter trajectories and greater penetration.

A hunter in camouflage hunting clothes pauses, with a compound bow in hand, to survey the countryside before continuing to stalk his prey. The compound bow is now the most popular hunting bow in the United States.

Introduction

Medieval archers attack at the 601st anniversary of the Battle of Grunwald on July 16, 2011, in Grunwald, Poland. The event attracted 4,000 reenactors, 1,200 knights, and 20,000 spectators.

The engineering description of the draw cycle of a bow (pulling the bowstring to full draw) is called a draw-force curve. It charts draw weight in pounds on the vertical Y-axis by draw length in inches on the horizontal X-axis. For a stick bow, the cycle approximates a gently curving line at about 45 degrees. The farther it is drawn, the greater the energy that is stored, and the stiffer the resistance and the more difficult it is to hold. For a compound bow, the chart resembles a bell curve: the bowyer draws at first with some difficulty, but when the pulleys (cams or wheels) rotate at the top of the bell, the effort to hold at full draw is quickly reduced.

At full draw, for instance, of a modern 70-pound compound bow advertised with either 65 percent or 80 percent let-off (the drop in holding weight after the pulleys roll over) will have a holding weight of either 24.5 or 14 pounds, respectively. Because holding these weights is much easier than holding 70 pounds, the archer can regulate his breathing and concentrate longer on his sights and the target.

The compound bow is much easier to shoot effectively than a stick bow, so the entry-level learning curve is shorter and the requirement to continually practice is lower. Whether inventor Holless Allen was thinking of this as he developed the compound bow in the 1960s is unknown, but he was granted a U.S. patent for the concept in 1969.

Since the compound bow's creation and the many contributions made to its development since then, it has become the bow of choice in the United States where archery is dominated by hunting and hunting-themed shooting events. Today more than three million archers shoot with compound bows whereas, according to best industry estimates, a few hundred thousand shoot stick bows. The number of crossbow hunters is unknown, but rising rapidly as states open big game seasons for crossbows.

Although the compound bow is shot in almost every nation, outside the United States its popularity is limited to small pockets of hunting and competition. Because the modern compound bow is a complex system of cables and pulleys, and because it requires specialty arrows and other accessories such as plastic fletching, sights, stabilizers, complex arrow rests, and mechanical release aids, it often lacks the commercial and informational support structure that is present in the thousands of widely available sporting goods stores and pro shops in the United States.

There is also a tendency in archery to venerate the traditional methods and tools. Archery, like fencing or hatchet throwing, is an archaic pastime practiced now

Members of an historical archery club shoot on target at Festival Cerveny Kamen 2010 in Cerveny Kamen, Slovakia.

New world champion Denisse Astrid Van Lamoen from Chile at the World Archery Championships, July 10, 2011, in Turin, Italy

for its own sake rather than because one must feed a family or go to war with the bow and arrow, spear, and atlatl.

Accessories for Archery

Archery is very basic: stick, string, arrow.

Yet the actual operation of a bow and arrow to accomplish any meaningful task requires a host of accessories. Today there are scores of accessories and styles that make outfitting an archer a thing of practical beauty, and accessories can be as simple and inexpensive as the poorest outdoorsman could wish, or just as impossibly expensive.

The earliest archers understood accessories. For example, an arrow could not be just any stick in the forest. Shafts were carefully selected for strength and straightness. The first archers learned to notch their arrows to fit against the string, perhaps with a flint knife, and to attach bird feathers for guidance.

The business end of early arrows might only have

Brady Ellison from the USA competes for a bronze medal at the 2011 World Archery and Para Archery Championships, July 10, 2011, in Turin, Italy.

been fire-hardened, killing from the shock of impact. Men must quickly have discovered that sharp bone or rock tips helped bring down game. And when they understood penetration, they needed binding and glue, perhaps boiled animal intestines, to secure the arrowhead on the shaft.

After men began to rely on the bow for their food and protection, their interest in accessories surely increased. Men quickly advanced from carrying arrows in their hands to carrying them in bark or animal-skin quivers holding a dozen shafts. Feathers tied to the bow helped calculate wind direction.

Perhaps the first truly useful accessory was the thumb ring. Archers using a thumb draw, in which the thumb hooks around the string beneath the arrow, found that rings of stone, antler, or leather protected the pad of the thumb, especially when shooting multiple arrows from heavy bows. From that point, thousands of years ago, the sky was the limit for accessories.

Arrow

Shooting a bow without an arrow may result in catastrophic damage to the bowman: a cracked limb, a broken string, or a bloody nose. The arrow is fundamental to archery. Yet the difficulty that troubled the first archer still bedevils shooters of today, that is, making the arrow fly straight.

Wood arrows are readily available in cedar, even poplar. They are traditional, with an exquisite appeal to lovers of the poetry of stick and string art. Archers who shoot longbows and recurves usually shoot wood arrows, but wood is inadequate for bows made of high-energy compounds, because wood has inconsistent internal structure. It is thus almost impossible to match spine, stiffness, and weight of a wood arrow with consistent accuracy over the distance required for high-performance shooting.

Modern compound bows store tremendous amounts of energy and thus high-performance archers have turned to hollow aluminum or fiberglass—often called "carbon"—tubing. Easton developed the original aluminum performance arrow. For 50 years, an Easton shaft was the world standard. The company's shafts could be produced with super-fine tolerances and in many sizes, colors, and degrees of stiffness. Once bent, however, aluminum shafts were difficult to straighten and could never again fly perfectly true.

Aluminum, therefore, gave way to carbon as the material used for most shooting and hunting arrows. Although carbon is more expensive, its manufacture could match the precision of aluminum. Plus, carbon has one characteristic that aluminum lacks: memory. A carbon shaft can bend and then self-align; it is tougher to damage than an aluminum shaft.

Crossbow terminology sometimes refers to arrows as bolts. Bolts or arrows are propelled along a track, but flight dynamics still require a clean release of a balanced and stabilized arrow for a good shot.

The Arrow's Butt

Arrows are built on shafts. At the rear, a nock holds the arrow on the bowstring, gripping without being tight. Historically, nocks were made from bone or horn, but today's nocks are plastic and mount either directly to a shaft or to a special insert.

Crossbow bolts do not use string-pinching nocks. The butt of a bolt may be flush or have a shallow,

Early in the twentieth century, archery was the first Olympic sport to admit women competitors.

semicircular groove. An arrow on a vertical bow only touches the string and the rest, but crossbow arrows slide in a track or groove until they fly free.

Excellent arrow flight requires the arrow shaft to spin because the spinning stabilizes the arrow. This is accomplished by gluing feathers to the rear of the shaft. Feathers cause friction so that the rear of the shaft drags, and differences in air pressure on the sides of the feathers result in spin so that the heavier fore-end with the arrowhead stabilizes and the arrow flies true.

Today, feathers have, by and large, been replaced by soft plastic vanes, but the merits of the material from which the vane is made are hotly debated. Some archers even substitute a rigid plastic for the soft plastic, but the most common set-up is a shaft with three aligned vanes attached, or fletched, in a helical pattern.

The Arrow's Point

The fore-end of a shaft delivers the arrow point. The manufacturing of points from stone—the earliest points made—was once a skilled operation, now called knapping. Not every type of stone has an internal structure that flakes when struck by another stone or when force is applied with the tip of an antler.

A garpoon point is used in bowfishing. When the target is hit, the collar is pushed back and the barbs spring out, locking into the fish.

Thus, the best, and most commonly used, stones for making arrow points were flint, obsidian, and quartz. Produced one at a time by hand, stone points had excellent cutting and penetrating abilities.

When men began working with metal, they realized a bonanza. Metal could not only serve for building arrowheads, it could also be mass-produced in a variety of forms, not just what the rock and the craftsman's eye allowed. Heads of bronze and iron replaced stone as civilization advanced beyond tribal societies. But unlike inherently sharp stone flakes, metal heads needed continual sharpening.

Formerly, arrowheads were blunts for practice and small game, field points for practice or competition, or broadheads for hunting. Whereas blunts and field points remain little changed from their traditional forms, broadheads have undergone an evolutionary spiral in design and performance.

Broadheads are now of two types. Solid, fixed-blade heads with a flat, double-edged design have been the standard since time immemorial. Today, however, solid heads with two to six blades can be purchased in any archery shop. Traditional heads are a single piece and may be resharpened. Others, such as the Bear Razorhead, use small insert blades to widen the cut.

Newer model broadheads use surgically sharp, replaceable blades that insert into a steel-tipped aluminum ferrule, which screws into an insert glued into the arrow shaft. These blades may be resharpened and reused, but are most often discarded after one shot.

The revolution in broadheads has been the development of heads with blades that swing open upon impact. Because penetration, slicing, and bleeding are the requirements of a good shot, engineers have spent countless hours perfecting these systems. Such mechanical heads commonly incorporate two blades and have overcome early criticism that they penetrate poorly on angled shots.

The true benefit of a mechanical head is that, with blades locked in the ferrule, only minimal surface area

is susceptible to windplaning, which can cause erratic flight. Mechanicals do "fly like a field point" and, once deployed, the blades usually produce a wider cut than fixed heads.

In the Hand

Drawing and releasing a heavy bowstring with fleshy thumbs and fingers is fine—once—but repeating that process four or five times soon becomes quite painful. Thus, inventors reimagined the thumb ring, adding leather tabs and gloves for holding the string. A tab is the mark of Olympic-style competition.

Alternatively, modern archers can use a hand-held mechanical aid that secures the string to a metal hook. The hook is connected via a series of ball bearings, levers, and springs to a trigger. It can be hand held (competition) or incorporated into a wrist sling (hunting).

The beauty of a mechanical aid is a crisp release. With three fingers—typical for recurves, longbows, and lightweight compounds—the string is held by soft flesh, whereas with a mechanical release, the string is held by a metal 1/8-inch hook. When the trigger is

Target archery accessories have added to the recurve bow the same characteristics incorporated into the structure and design of a compound bow.

punched, the hook springs away instantly and arrow flight can practically be perfect. Crossbows operate in a similar manner, with the mechanical release incorporated into the stock.

On the Bow

In the stick bow era, an archer would lay the arrow on a padded bow shelf and draw the string with a leather tab or glove. The only accessory might have been a primitive sight, but that is no longer the case today. The bow's design and composition have changed so dramatically that Saxton Pope and Art Young might not even recognize a fully equipped modern bow.

The arrow rest, essential to holding the shaft until release, has progressed dramatically. Adjustability to fit the specific needs of the bowyer is now a standard feature. The current competition choice is a low-friction rest with stainless arms to hold the arrow, but hunter rests have become engineering marvels. State-of-the-art hunting rests now support the arrow until the instant after release, then drop out of the way of the vanes that can travel in excess of 300 feet per second. Contact between the rest and the vanes can throw the arrow off course.

Sights, too, have undergone a major upgrade. Early archers shot instinctively, living and sometimes dying by their bows. Now, archery is more often a hobby, and accurate instinctive shooting is rare.

The major development in sighting over the last 25 years is the incorporation of fiber optic technology. Tru-Glo promoted fiber optics in archery, but many companies now market this brilliant technology. A fiber optic cord built into a sight pin gathers light and gives archers a tiny bright point of reference for aiming. Using fiber optics with an adjustable, battery-powered glow light allows superb aiming in any light conditions.

To help balance and dampen the movement of the bow—a bow jumps forward when the string is released—archers screw stabilizers into a mounting plug below the grip. A stabilizer is more than simply the addition of solid weight. It often incorporates dampening materials to reduce the noise and vibration of a shot. Because the bows of today can shoot at an arrow speed above 400 feet per second, rubberized dampening materials are now widely distributed on the limbs and string and are even attached to other accessories such as the bow-mounted quiver, rest platform, and bow sight.

The art of archery is all about hitting the bull's-eye, whether that is a gold ring or the vitals of a big game animal. Today, more than ever, a plethora of accessories is available to speed the arrow on its course.

An archer prepares to release the bowstring. He is using sophisticated balancing equipment to improve his aim and hit the bull's-eye on his target.

AMS Bowfishing

AMS Bowfishing, located in Stratford, Wisconsin, carries a broad array of archery-related equipment. The company offers retriever reels; bowfishing bows; big game equipment; crossbow equipment; arrows, points, and slides; apparel; a wide range of accessories; and replacement parts. The company's crossbow equipment and big game equipment include gator kits, and arrows especially made to hunt tiger sharks are also part of the AMS product line.

Up to date with social media, the company has its own Facebook page that updates friends and the public with news about upcoming bowfishing competitions and championships. In addition, webisodes of bowfishing sorties all around the nation are posted regularly. Recently posted webisodes have been filmed in Tennessee, California, Illinois, South Dakota, and Wisconsin. The excitement and thrill of the hunt keeps viewers on the edge of their seats!

AMS Bowfishing is a private company established in 1997. The company sponsors an annual bowfishing competition called the AMS Bowfishing Big 30 Challenge.

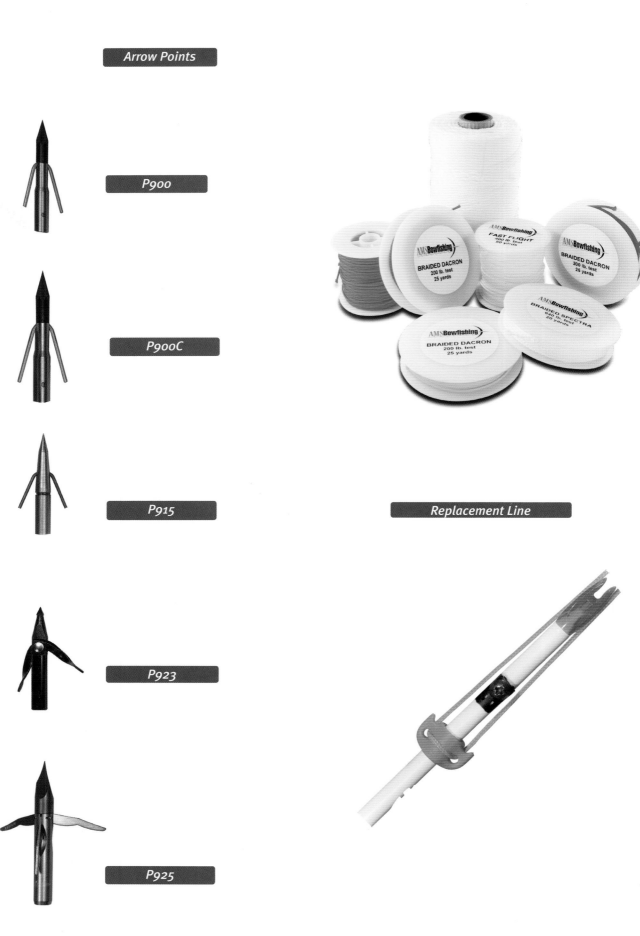

Arrow Points

P900

P900C

P915

P923

P925

Replacement Line

Safety Slides

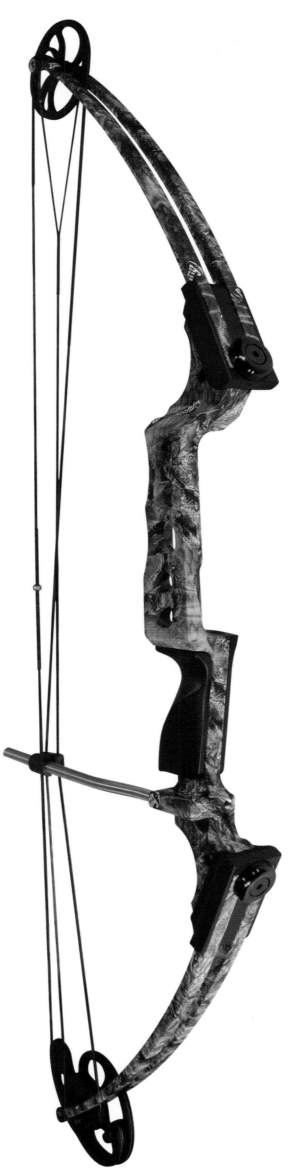

Fish Hawk Bow with Koi Carp Camo

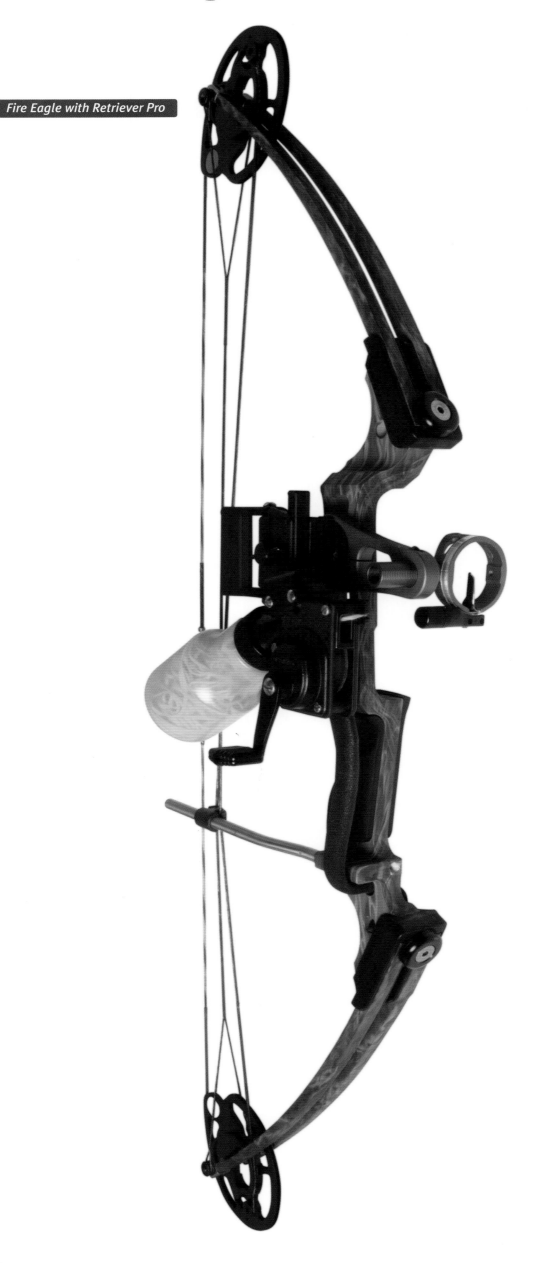

Fire Eagle with Retriever Pro

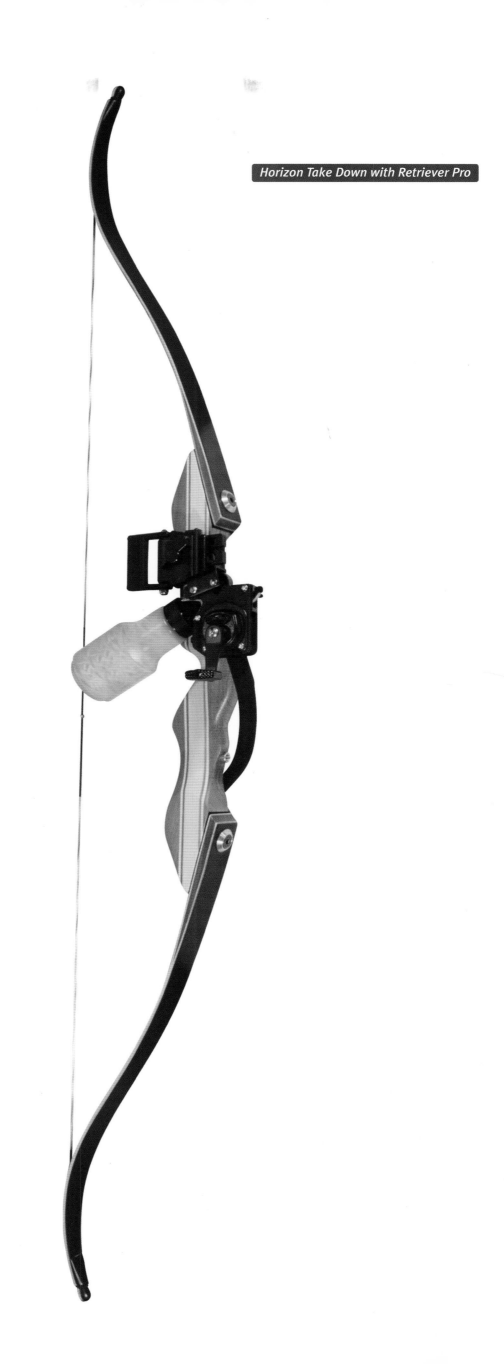

AMS Bowfishing

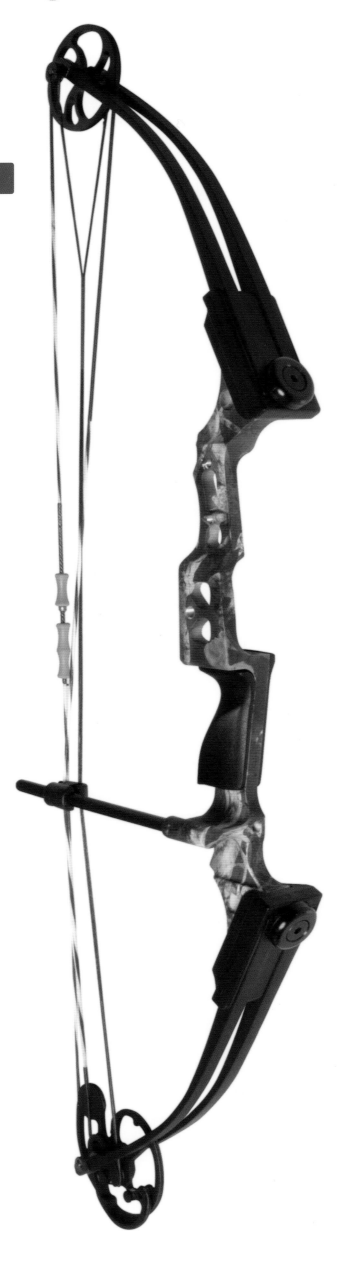

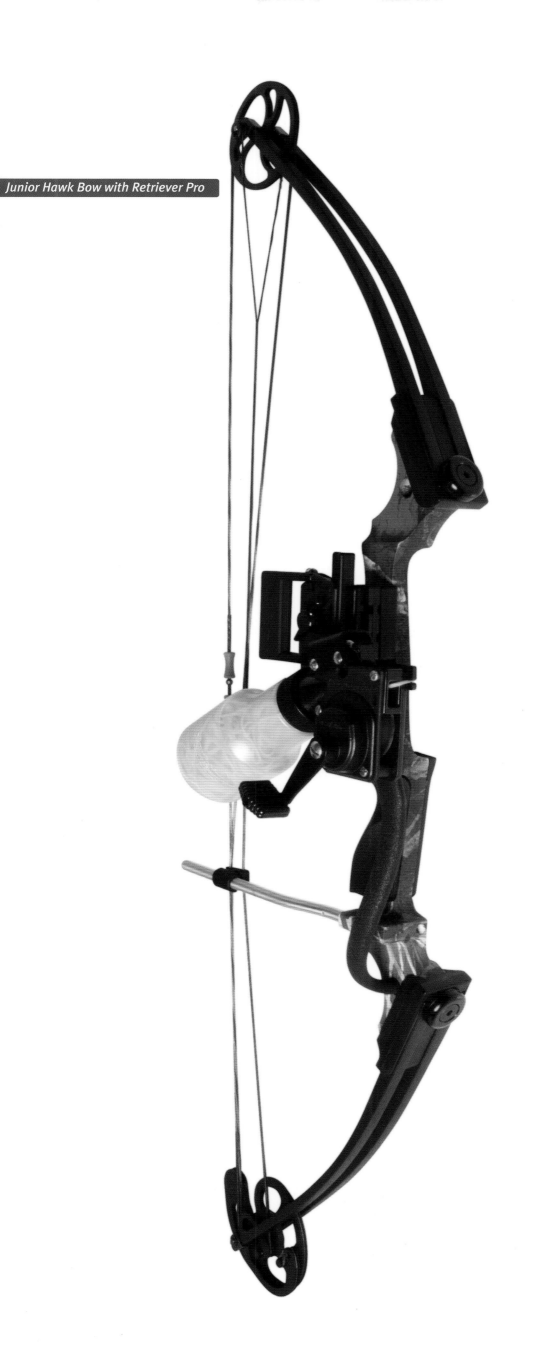

Bear Archery

Bear Archery, located in Evansville, Indiana, sells compound bows, traditional archery equipment, apparel, youth archery sets, institutional equipment, and a wide spectrum of archery-related accessories. A truly modern company, Bear Archery spreads its message and grows its community on Facebook, Twitter, and YouTube.

Legendary sportsman Fred Bear always said: "It's all about the hunt. Your hunt." Bear Archery continues to embrace that sentiment through its continued focus on quality in both design and workmanship.

Fred Bear was born in Waynesboro, Pennsylvania, in 1902. At the age of 21, Fred moved to Detroit to pursue a career in the growing auto industry. There he was inspired by the film *Alaskan Adventure,* a documentary on the bow-hunting adventures of Art Young. Soon Fred was learning to make his own bows, arrows, and bowstrings and was being taught by Young himself.

Fred opened Bear Products in 1933, but its primary business was advertising and silk-screening for automakers; bows were just a sideline he made mainly for himself and friends. By 1940, Fred was fully immersed in all aspects of bow hunting and decided that same year to launch Bear Archery. He later made a series of films on bow hunting in the wild. On one of these expeditions, Fred downed an African bull elephant with a bow. *Life* magazine eventually featured Fred Bear and his hunting accomplishments in an article that further raised his stature around the world.

Bear Archery prides itself on the state-of-the-art technology that it uses to design and build its bows. Although the company's family of bows has always been of the highest quality, the company is not content to recycle old technology. Bear engineers continuously update the technology the company uses in order to make its bows lighter, stronger, faster, and quieter. Anarchy, the company's flagship bow, is not the only bow to incorporate the latest technology; all of the Bear bows benefit from advances in bow engineering technology.

Bear strives to develop cams that produce a smoother draw and release, faster speeds, and a more solid wall—and a lighter cam too! Technological advances are obvious not only in the Bear bow cams, but in the limb cup, grip design, riser, quad limbs, string suppressors, and roller guards. The 2012 Bear line of bows includes the Anarchy, Carnage, Mauler, Legion, Encounter, Outbreak, Siren, Home Wrecker, and Apprentice 2.

The Bear Archery website boasts numerous webisodes for both the devoted archery enthusiast and the beginner. Subjects of webisodes range from personal interest stories to educational hunting topics to instructional product explanations.

Anarchy

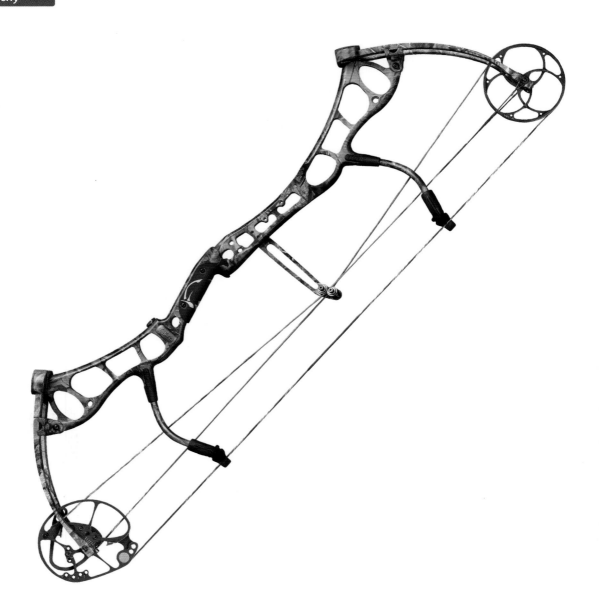

Apprentice 2

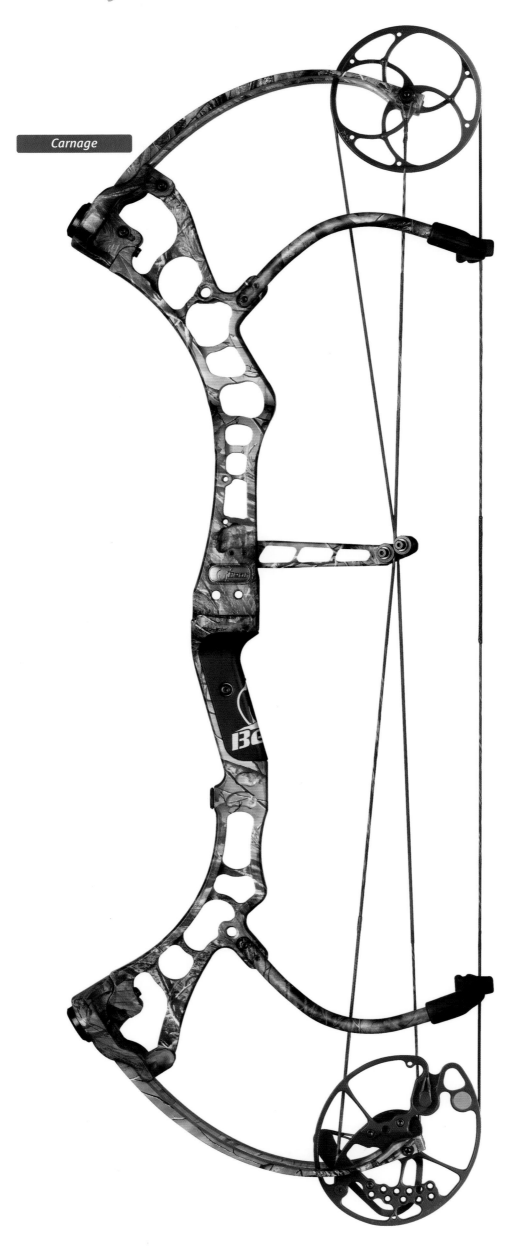

Carnage

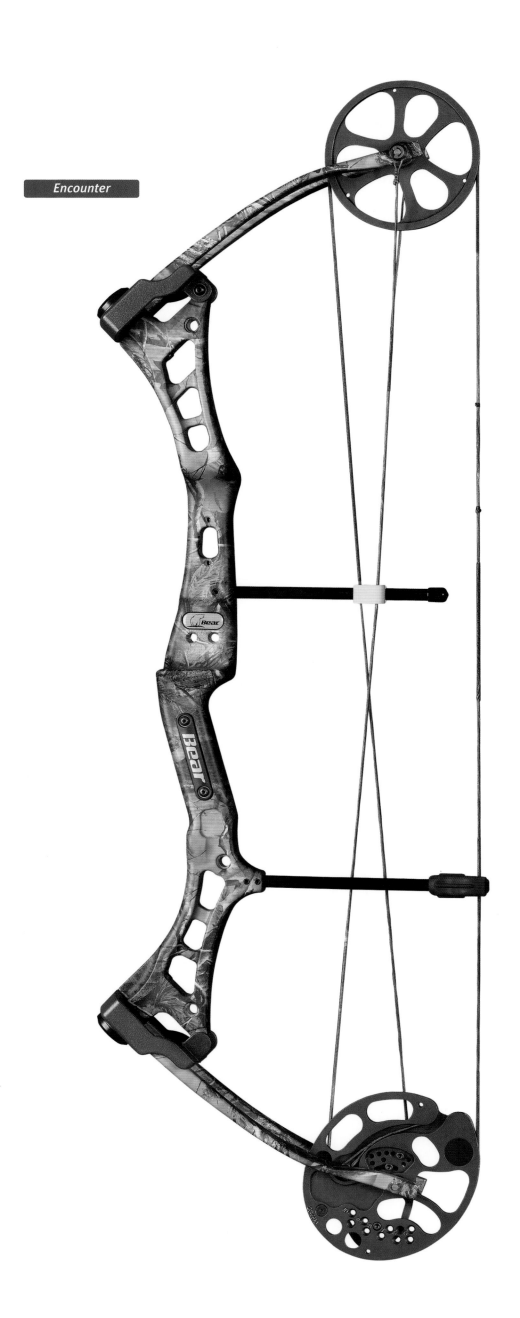

Encounter

Bear Archery

Home Wrecker

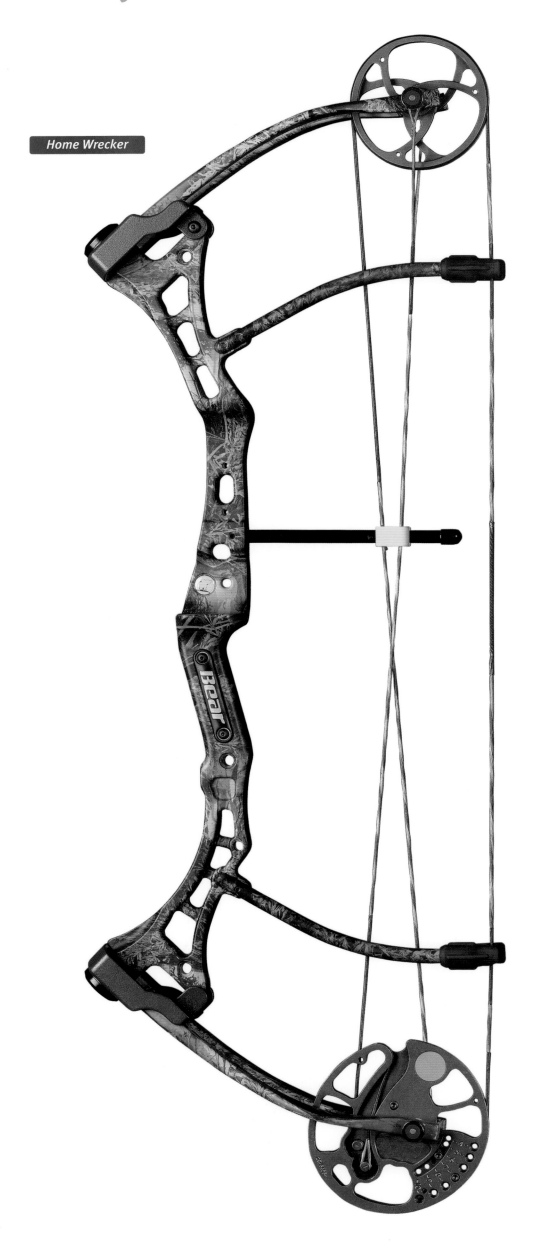

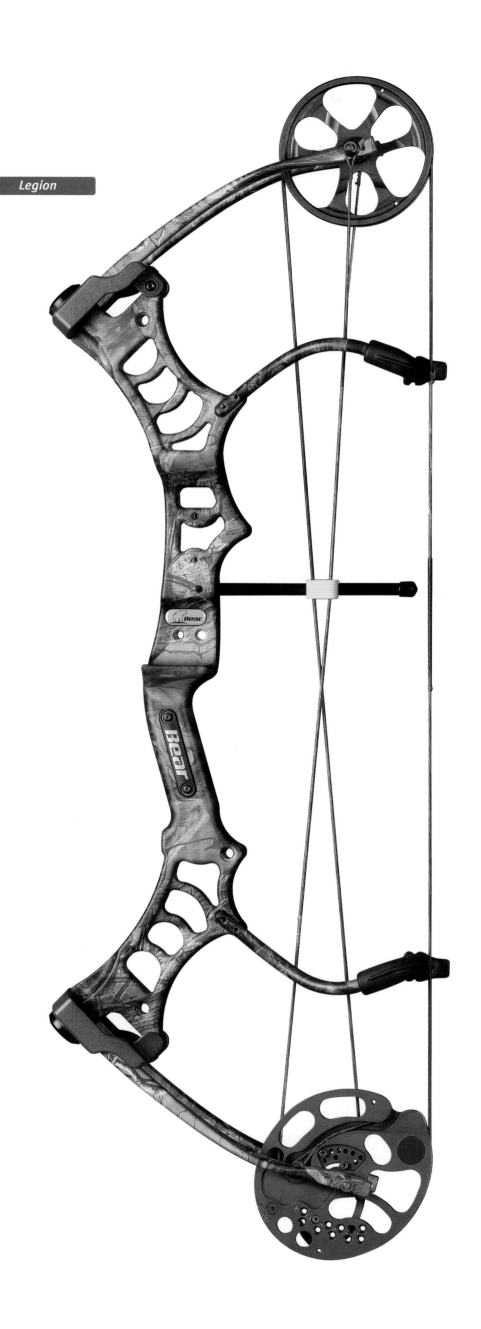

Legion

Bear Archery

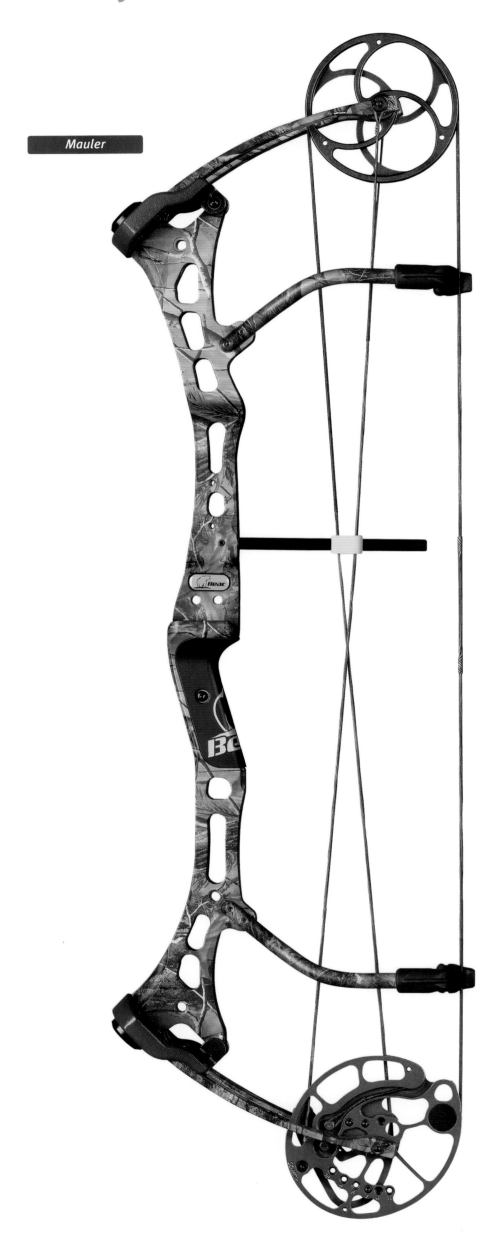

Mauler

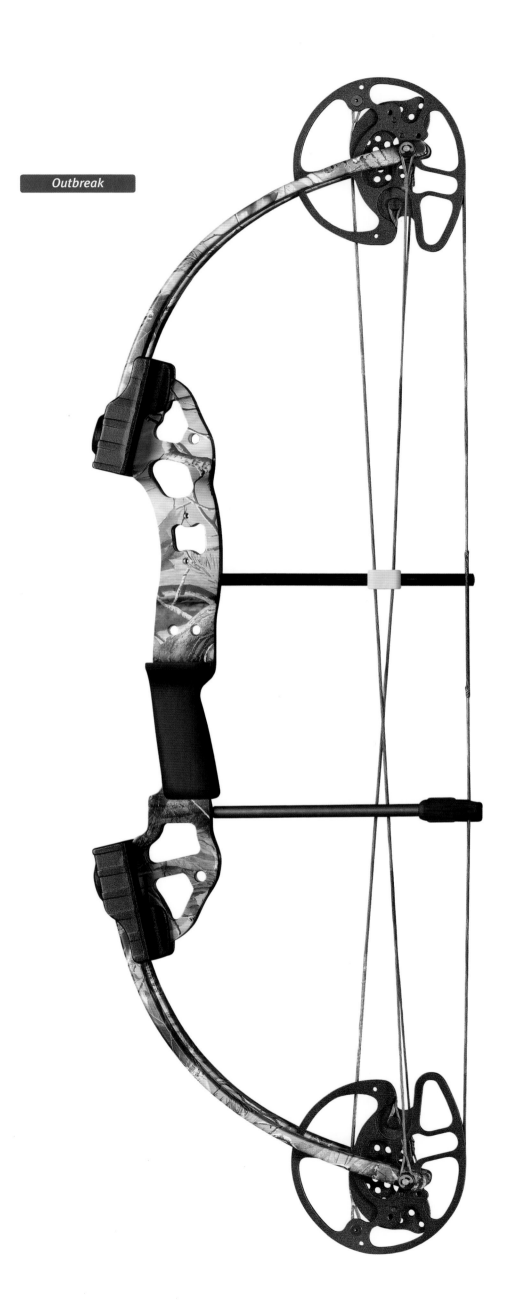

Outbreak

Siren

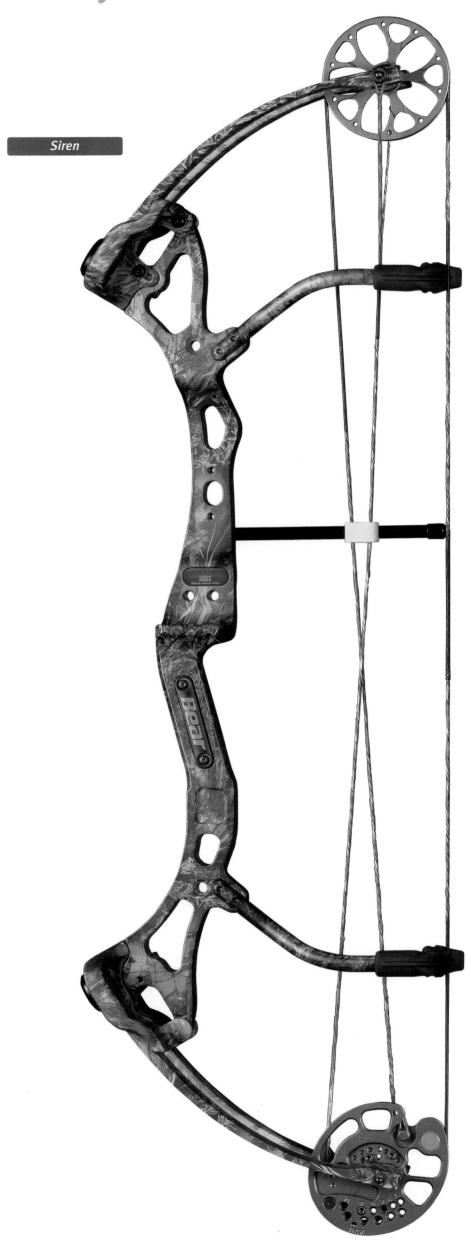

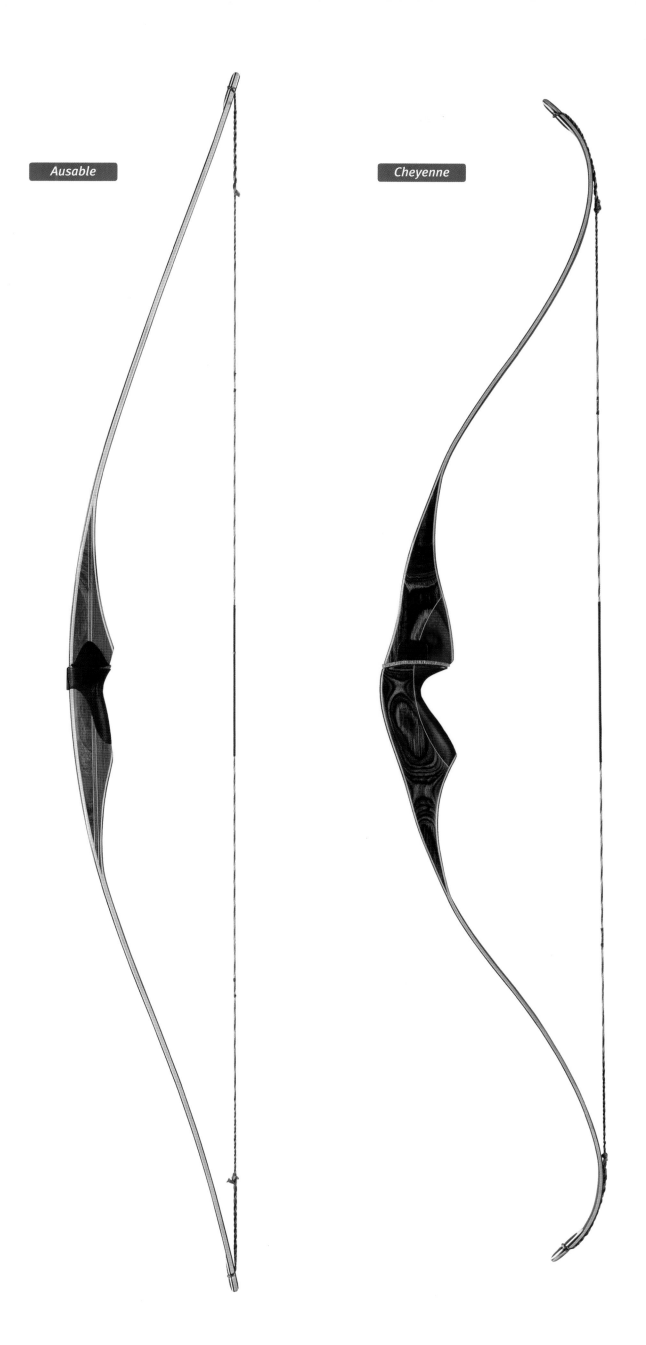

Ausable

Cheyenne

Bear Archery

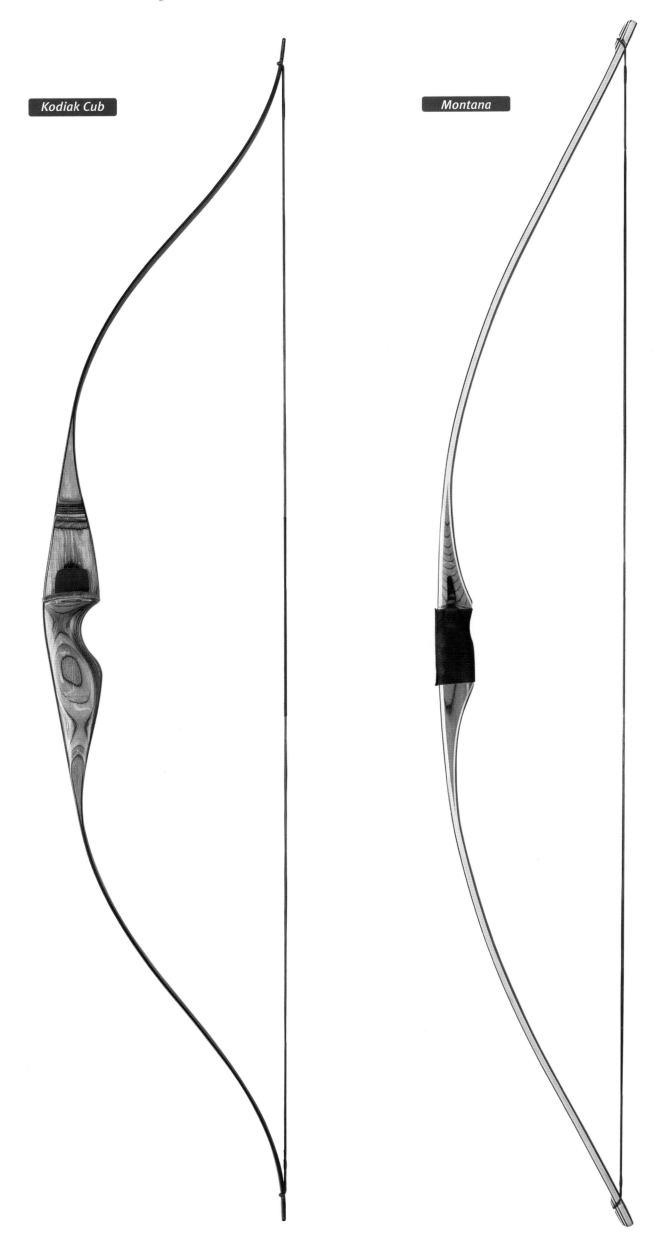

Kodiak Cub

Montana

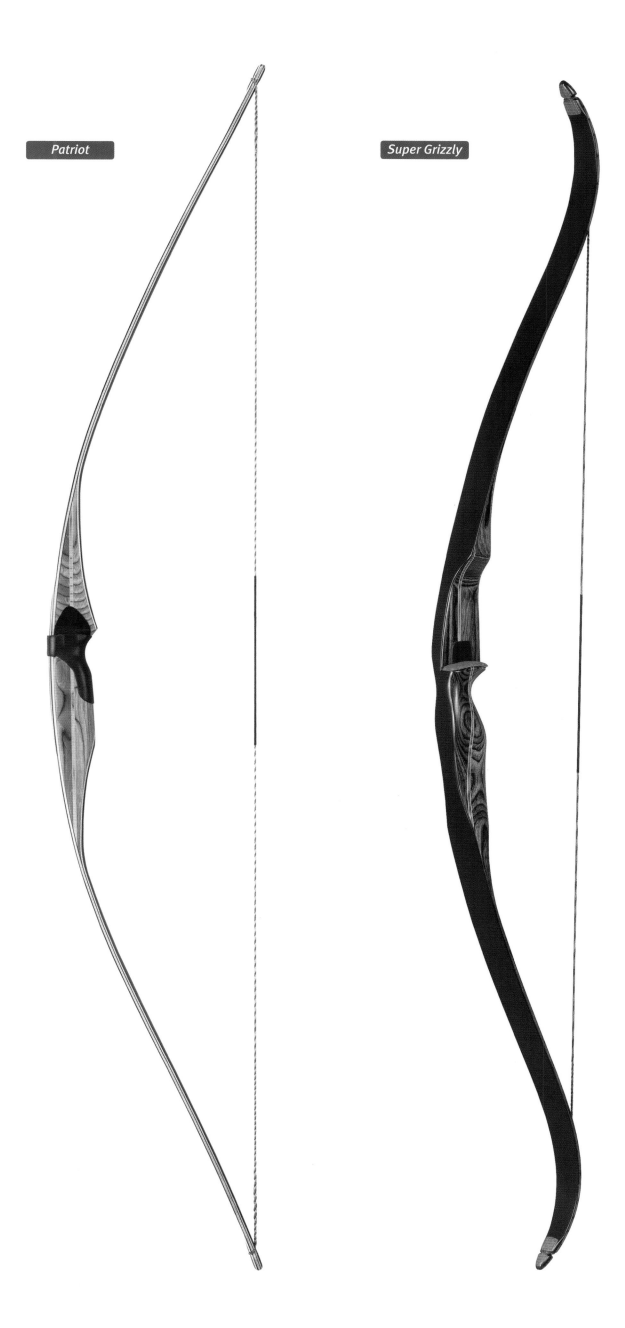

Patriot

Super Grizzly

Bear Archery

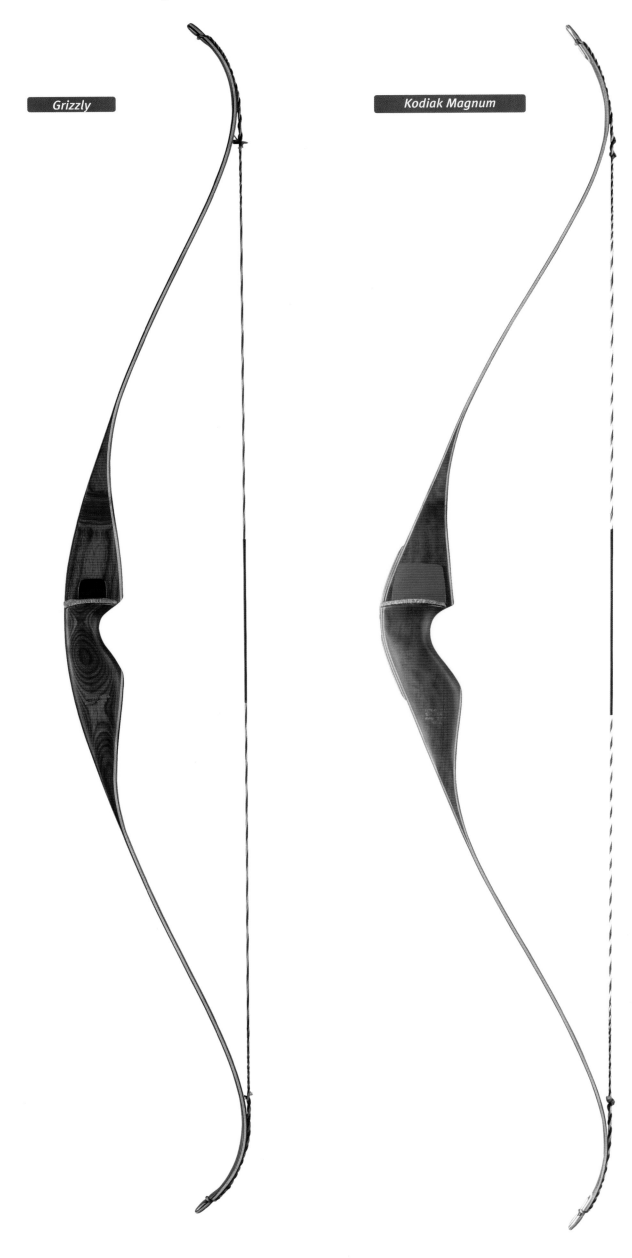

Grizzly

Kodiak Magnum

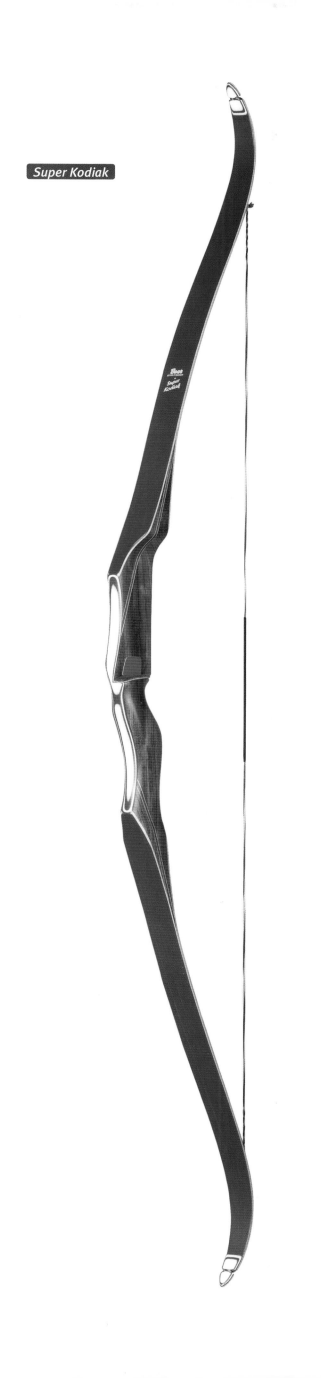

Super Kodiak

Bear Archery

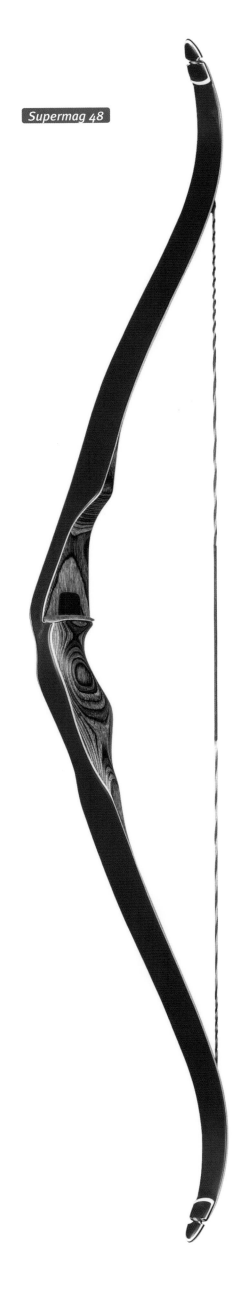

Supermag 48

Takedown

Excalibur Crossbows

Excalibur Crossbows is a crossbow-hunting business started by crossbow hunters. Bill and Kath Troubridge began their company in 1983 to make the most efficient, reliable, and accurate hunting crossbows that money can buy. They rely on their experience rather than engineers for designing and building their crossbows. The owners themselves subject each new design and reconfiguration to strenuous, real-world testing.

Excalibur guarantees that every bow it produces is capable of shooting groups of three inches or less at 25 yards using broadheads. The company attributes its ability to make this claim to its bows' recurve limbs, which are much faster than compound systems and have a fraction of their weight, noise, or mechanical failures, as well as to the trigger mechanism on its bows and the composite and aluminum stock that is virtually indestructible.

The Excalibur crossbow line includes the Eclipse XT, Ibex SMF, Equinox, Exomax, Vortex, Exocet 200, Phoenix, Axiom SMF, Pixel, Vixen II, and Apex as well as accessories for each.

A sense of community is promoted in several ways by the company. The website has a forum for crossbow enthusiasts to share information, ask questions, and engage other enthusiasts. Excalibur also has a Facebook page and produces an electronic newsletter, the Exblast. Kath Troubridge even posts wild game recipes for successful bow hunters!

Quiver

Firebolt Arrows

Boltcutter

Field Points

Exocet 200

Phoenix

Apex Target Crossbow

Excalibur Crossbows

Ibex SMF Kit

Exocet 200 Vari-Zone LSP

Exocet 200 Multi Red-Dot LSP

Equinox Vari-Zone LSP

X-ACT

Excalibur Crossbows

Vixen II Pink LSP

Ibex SMF Kit

Exocet 200 Shadow Zone LSP

Vortex Shadow Zone LSP

Eclipse XT Kit

Exomax Vari - Zone LSP

Excalibur Crossbows

Equinox

Exocet 200 Shadow Zone LSP

Exomax Multi Red Dot LSP

Axiom SMF Kit

Pixel Youth

Equinox Multi Red Dot LSP

Horton Archery

Horton Archery was born fifty years ago from the vision of Bernard Horton. The crossbow, which was once an important hunting tool in medieval times, gradually faded from use with the invention and development of the firearm, but its enduring allure spurred Bernard Horton, an accomplished gunmaker and avid sportsman, to devise innovations that have reinvigorated the crossbow's popularity as an effective short-range hunting tool.

The engineers at Horton Archery have been responsible for a number of technological innovations that include the Dial-A-Range rail design and many other pioneering features. Horton designs and builds custom-crafted crossbows for shooters of all ages and skill levels.

Horton's crossbows include the Fury, Havoc, Team Realtree, Bone Collector, The Brotherhood, Legacy CS 225, Scout 125, and Eagle. The Eagle is designed to meet the needs of children who are learning to bowhunt. Accessories in the Horton product line-up include arrows; scopes and sights; cocking devices; and noise and vibration control devices, among other items.

An interesting and useful feature of the company's website is their "News" tab under which are posted stories about pending crossbow-related legislation in the different American states, as well as updates on competitive events, archery season dates, training events, and technology news. Also on the company's website is a video library with short films on subjects such as proper cocking methods, sight systems, pre-shooting maintenance, and hunting safety guidelines.

The company is headquartered in Kent, Ohio. Find out more about Horton Archery on the company's Facebook page.

Bone Collector

Brotherhood Full Camo

Eagle

Fury

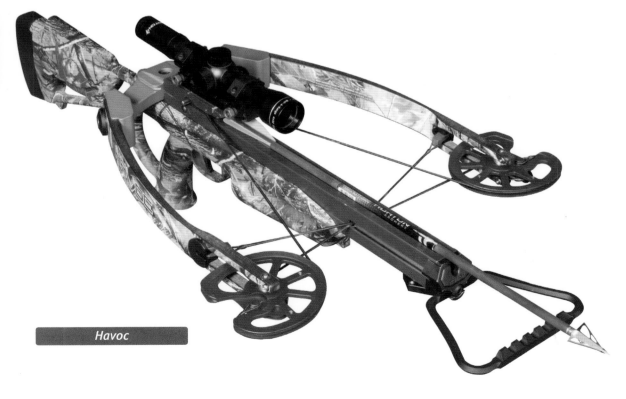

Havoc

Horton Archery

Legacy 175

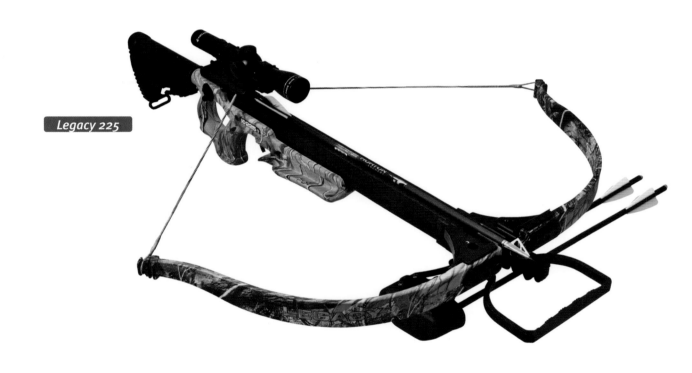

Legacy 225

Scout 125

Horton Archery

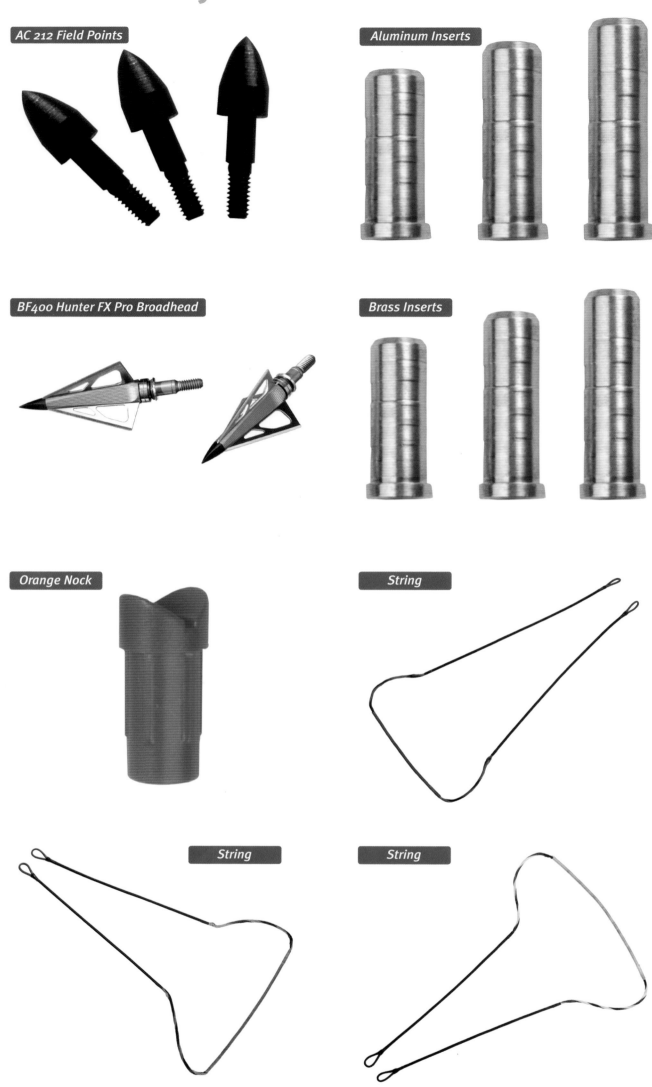

AC 212 Field Points

Aluminum Inserts

BF400 Hunter FX Pro Broadhead

Brass Inserts

Orange Nock

String

String

String

Bone Collector Arrow

Bone Crusher Arrow

Lightning Strike Arrow

*EZ Loader
Cocking
Rope w/Bridge*

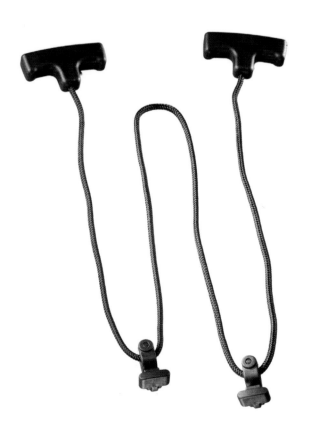

Martin Archery

Gail and Eva Martin started Martin Archery in 1951. After Gail's return from World War II, he rekindled his passion for archery and bowhunting. Three generations of the Martin family are now involved in the business. The first generation, that is, Gail, designs traditional bows and bowstrings. The second generation, Terry, focuses on compound designs, and the third generation, Ryan, promotes modern bow design.

Martin Archery's claim to fame is its longevity in the archery industry—61 years. Martin's line of compound bows includes the Pro Series, Gold Series, and Adventure Series. The traditional line of bows comprises the Gail Martin Recurve, Dream Catcher, Mamba, Hunter X-200, Bamboo Viper, Savannah, Adventure 2.0 54-inch, Explorer 68-inch, Saber Take-Down, and Jaguar Take-Down.

Because Martin Archery is a multigenerational family business, the company has a serious interest in engaging youths in the sport of archery and bowhunting. As a result, the company is proud of its high-performance and lightweight Tiger youth bow design. The Tiger offers a 10- to 20-pound draw weight and a sight window that allows for either right- or left-hand shooting. It has a 14- to 24-pound draw length.

Look for more information about Martin Archery on the company's Facebook page and follow the company's posts on Twitter. Walla Walla, Washington, is home to Martin Archery.

Bengal Pro

Tiger Youth Bow

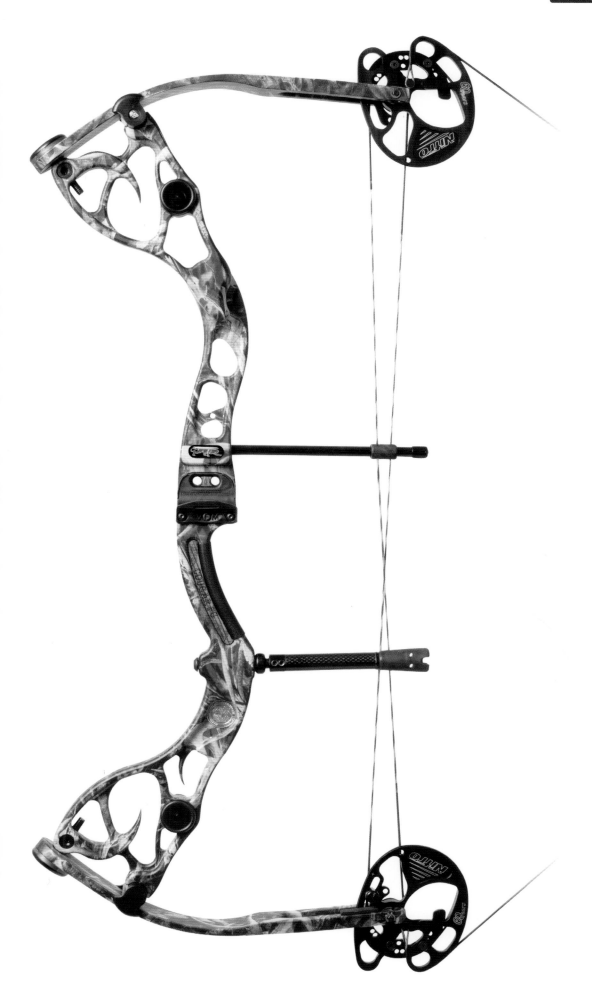

Martin Archery

Crossfire Pro Carbon

Exile Pro Carbon

Onza 3 Pro Red

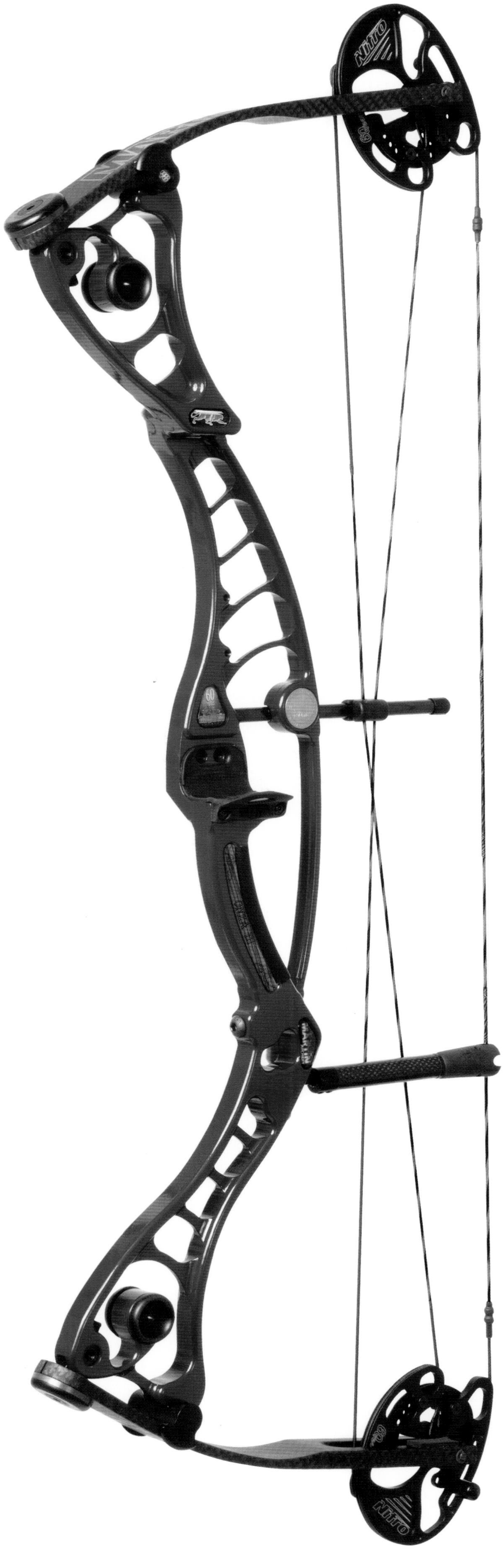

Pantera Vista

Martin Archery

Scepter V Pro

Silencer Carbon Fury XT

Martin Archery

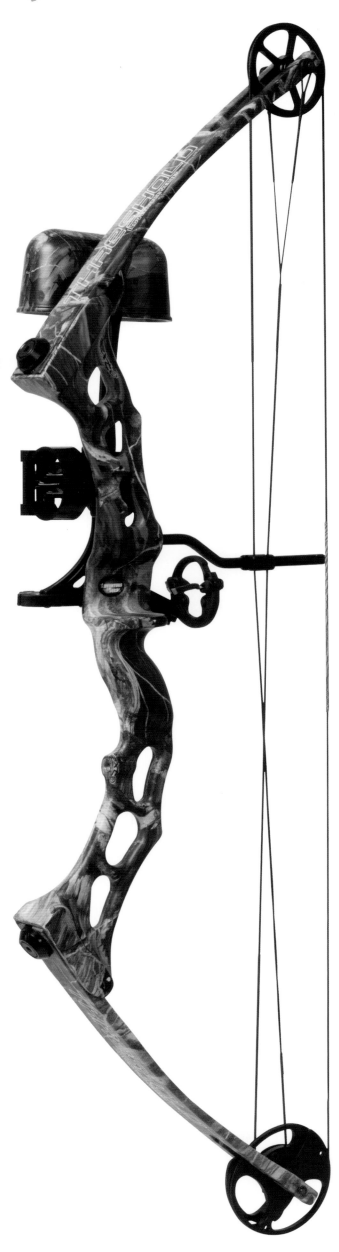

Threshold

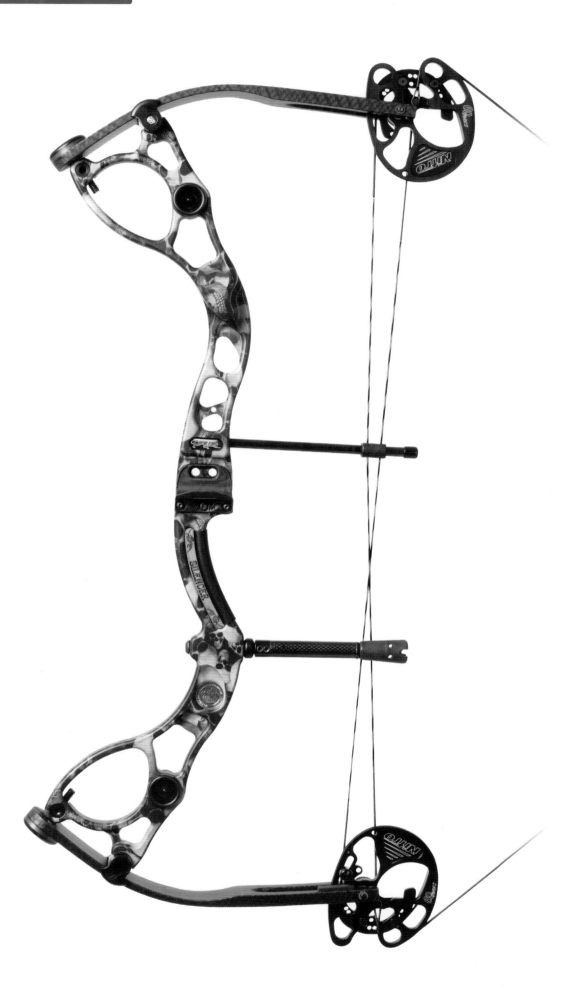

Martin Archery

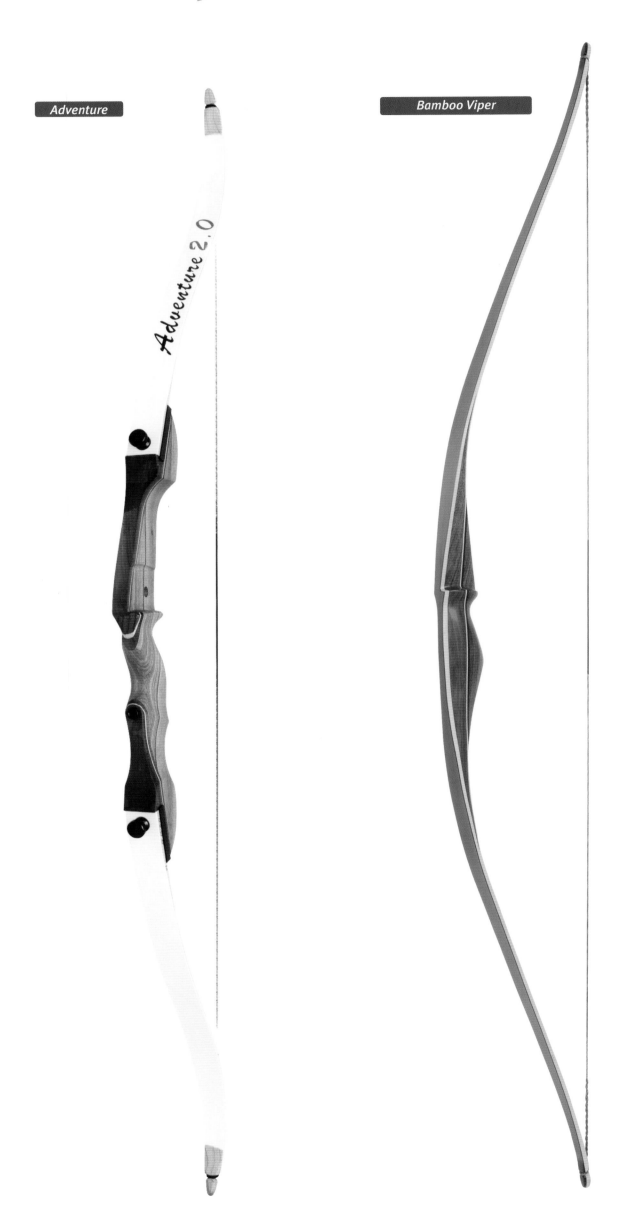

Adventure

Bamboo Viper

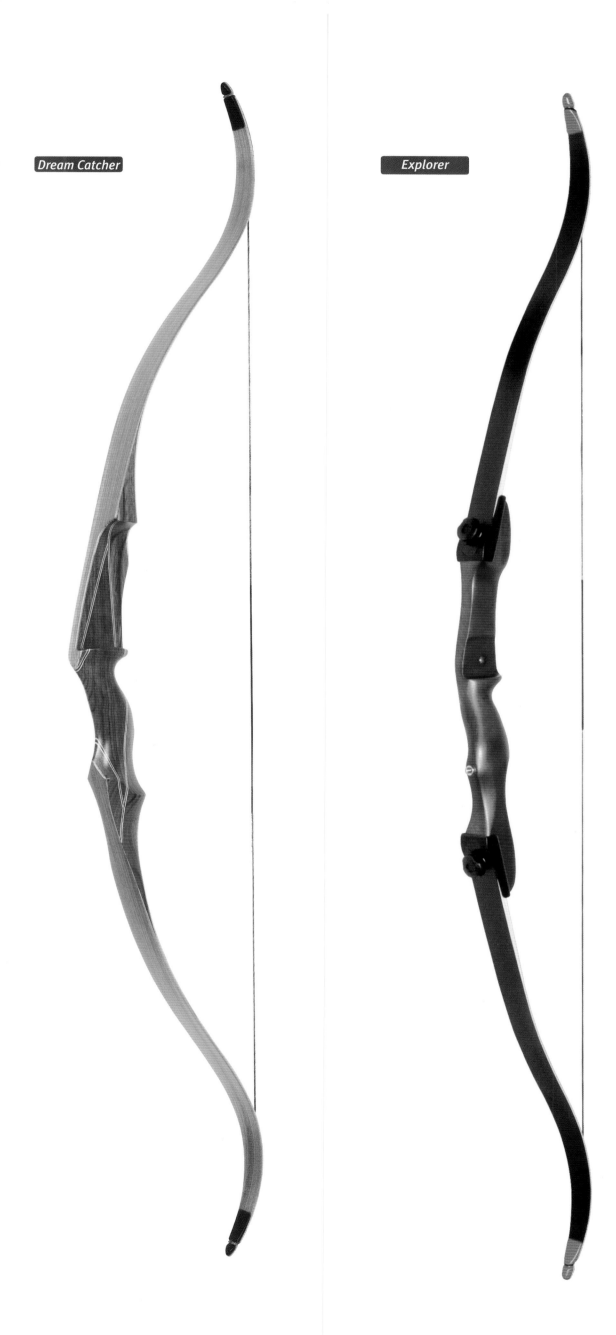

Dream Catcher

Explorer

Martin Archery

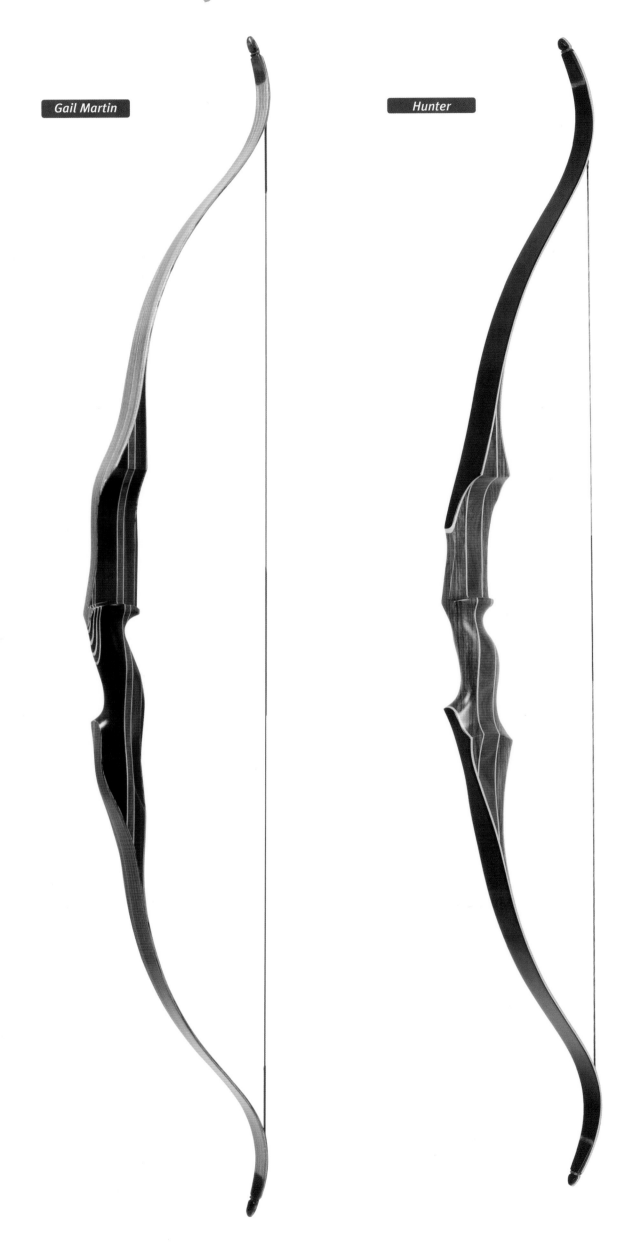

Gail Martin

Hunter

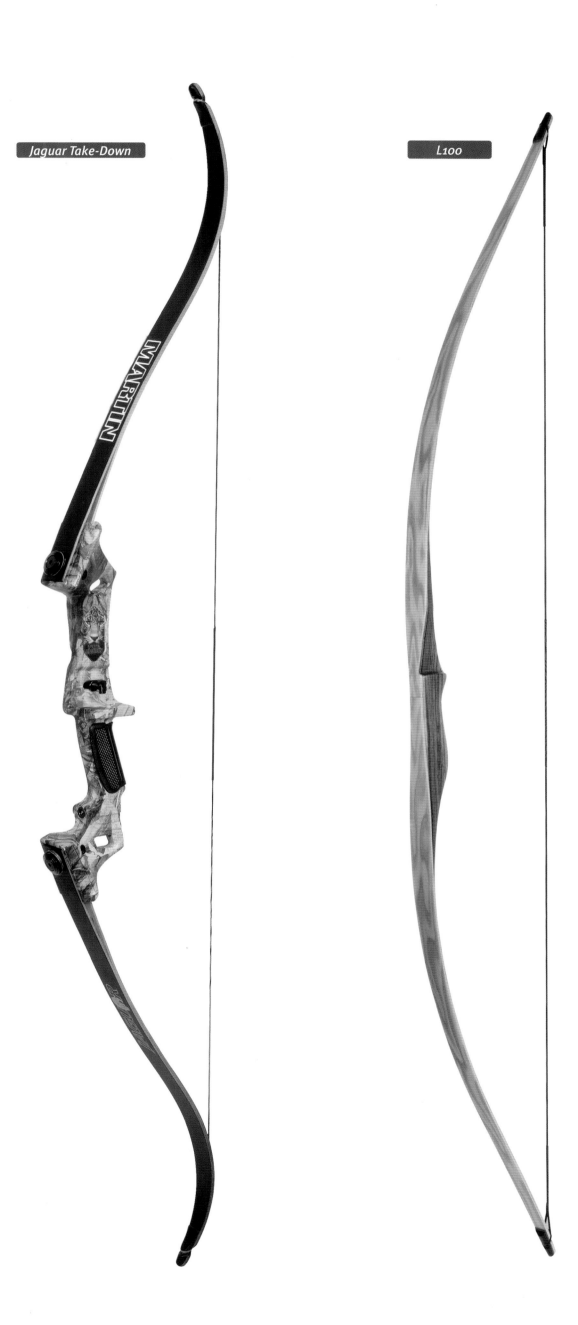

Jaguar Take-Down

L100

Martin Archery

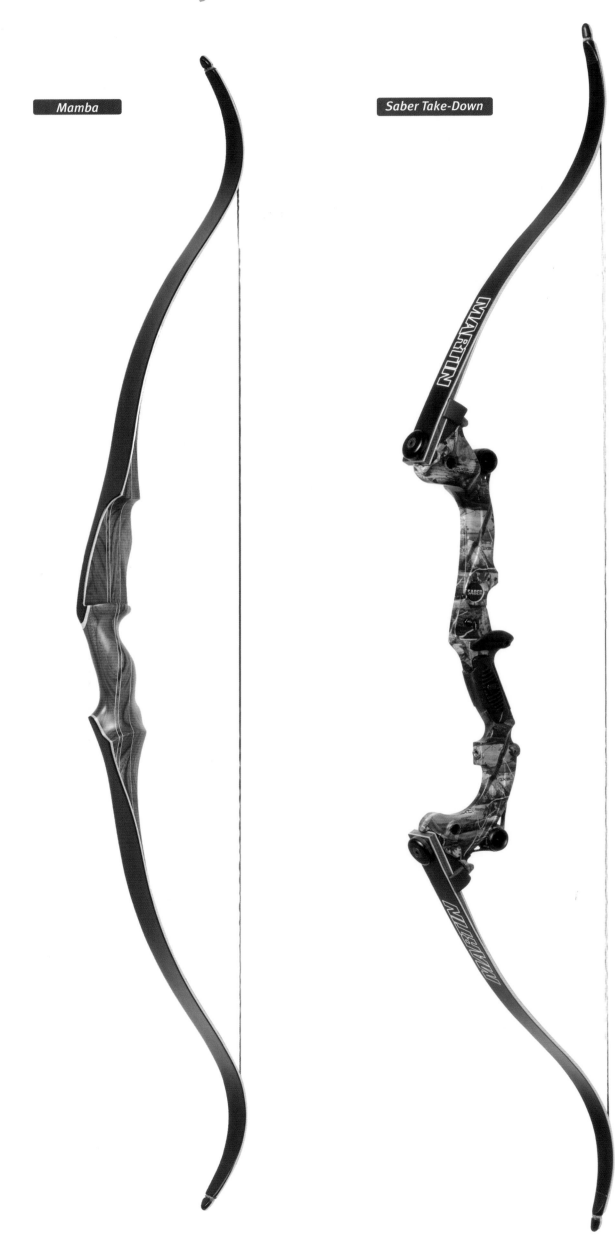

Mamba

Saber Take-Down

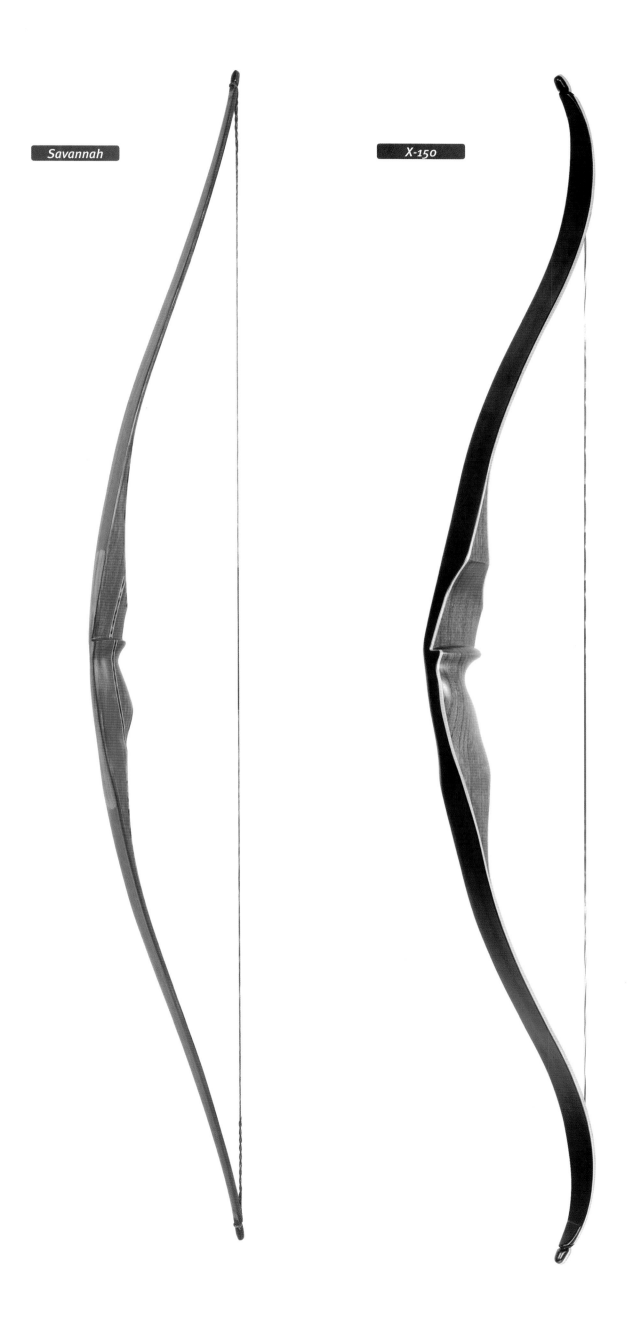

Savannah

X-150

Parker Bows

The state of Virginia is home to Parker Bows. Parker manufactures crossbows that range from speeds of 275 to 350 feet per second, as well as compound bows and accessories. All Parker bows are made in America and have a lifetime warranty for the original owner.

Parker Bows was started in 1984 by Robert Errett, who began his career working and hunting with Fred Bear at Bear Archery. Bob's first company was Nationwide Archery, which became Parker Bows in 2003, after which it assumed a more concentrated focus on compound bows. Twice in its history, Parker Bows has been named by *INC* magazine as one of the fastest-growing companies in America.

Parker's line of crossbows includes the Concorde, Gale Force, Tornado F4, Hornet Extreme, Tomahawk, Enforcer, Bushwacker, and Challenger. The company makes compound bows for youths as well as adults. The adult compound bow line comprises the Python, Inferno, Velocity, WildFire Extreme, and Blazer. The youth bow line includes the SideKick Extreme and BuckShot Extreme. Both brands are offered in a pink version.

In addition to a presence on Facebook and videos on YouTube, Parker's website is the place to view numerous crossbow safety and instructional videos.

Velocity

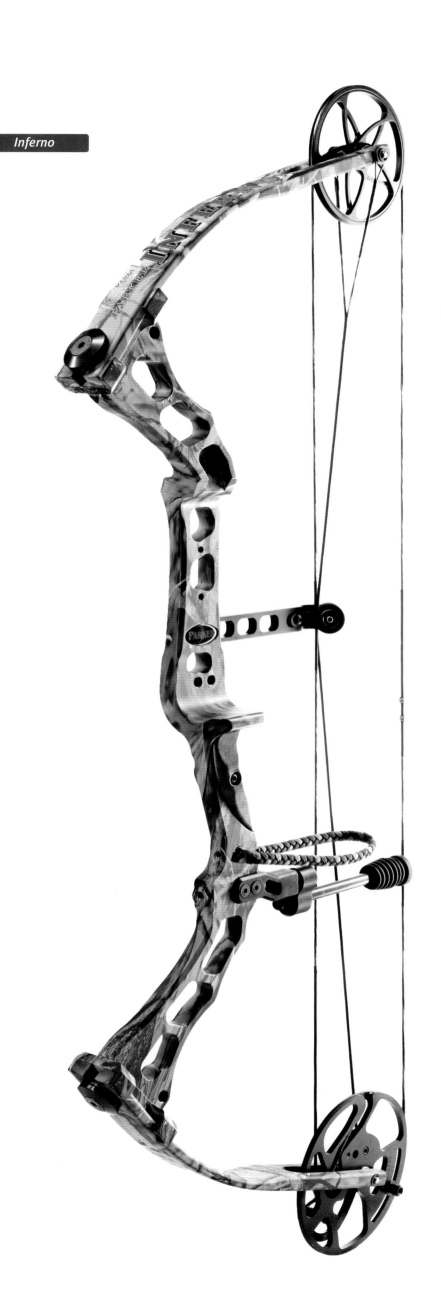

Parker Bows

Bushwacker

Bushwacker

Challenger

Concorde

Enforcer

Gale Force

Hornet Extreme

Parker Bows

Tornado F4

PSE Archery

PSE Archery was one of the first five companies to be licensed under the Allen patent for compound bows. PSE was started by Pete Shepley in Mahomet, Illinois. Before starting PSE, Pete worked for Magnavox as a product designer, spending his lunch hours perfecting the design of archery-related equipment. Today the company's claim to fame is being the largest privately owned archery equipment manufacturing company in the country.

The company's first compound bow was so successful when it was introduced at an archery tournament that within the following two weeks, 900 orders were received, simply by word of mouth or from seeing the bow in action. Located in Tucson, Arizona, PSE holds 20 patents for bow design and archery products. Its conviction that research and development is the key to making the industry grow has benefited its own products as well as those of its competitors.

The PSE Archery product line is extensive. It encompasses bows in the Pro Series (11 styles), Main Line (12 styles), Ready-to-Shoot (9 styles), Field-Ready (6 styles), Bow Fishing (2 styles), Longbows (4 styles), Recurve (16 styles), and Crossbows (6 styles). Accessories and apparel complete the company's product offerings.

The PSE Archery blog is a feature on the company's website

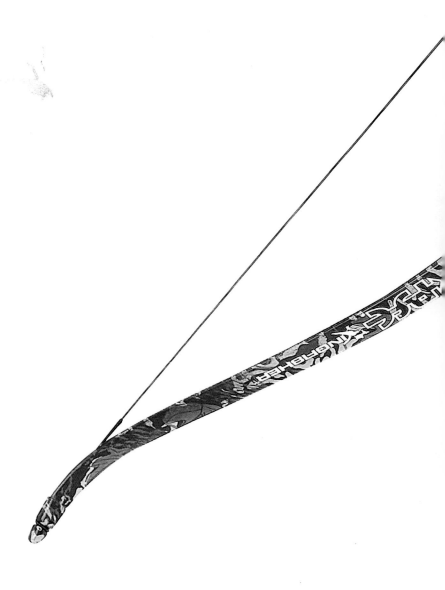

Kingfisher with reel

Copperhead TS

Crossfire XB

Foxfire

Reaper

Blackhawk

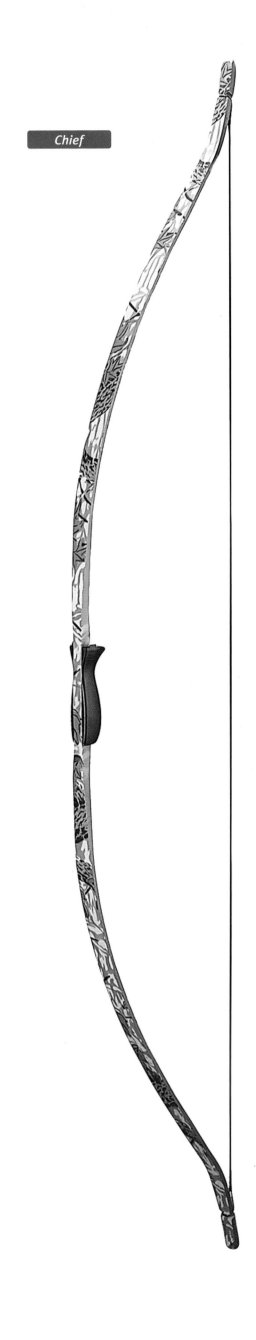

Chief

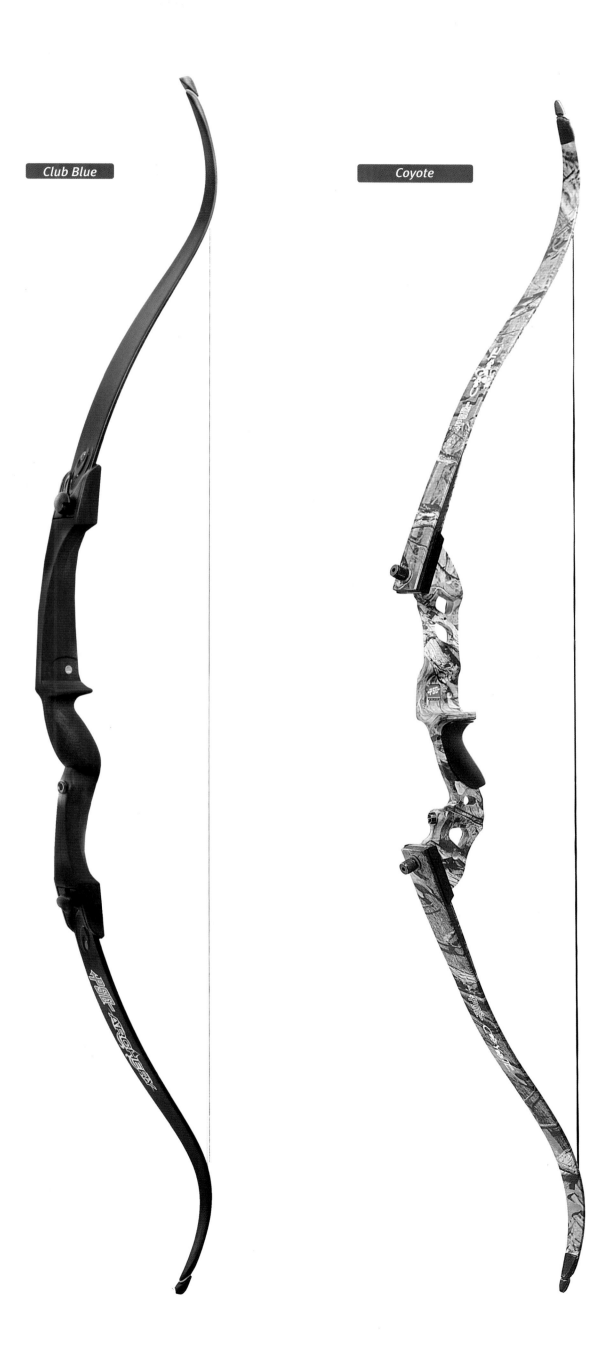

Club Blue

Coyote

PSE Archery

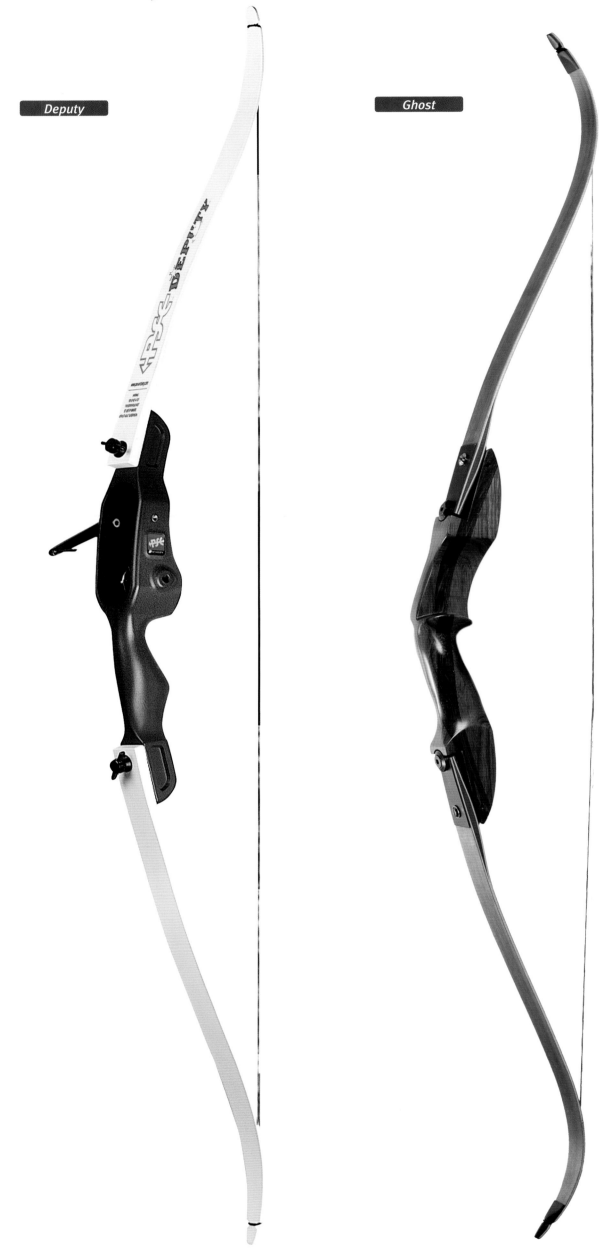

Deputy

Ghost

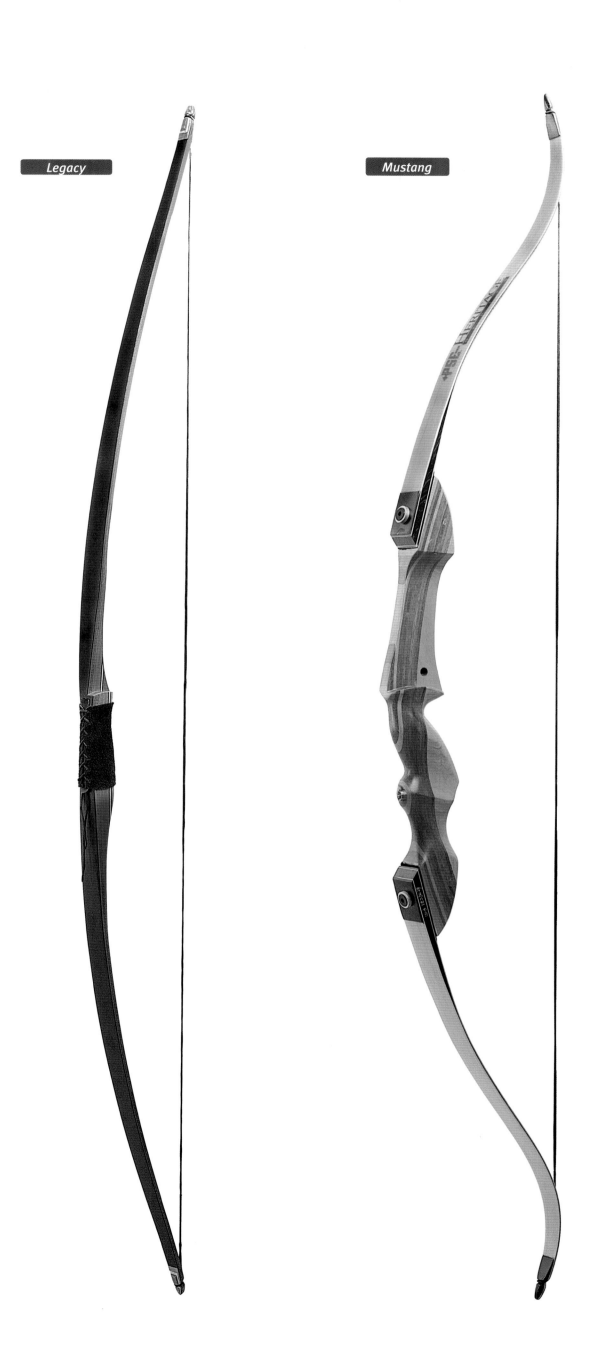

Legacy

Mustang

PSE Archery

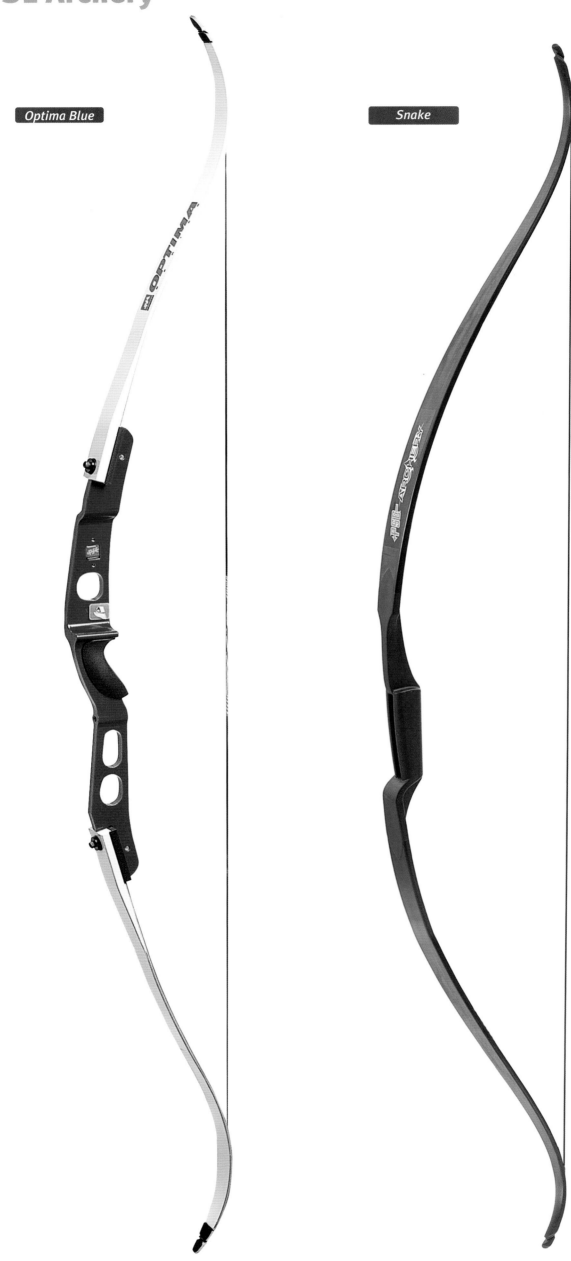

Optima Blue

Snake

Razorback

Sequoia

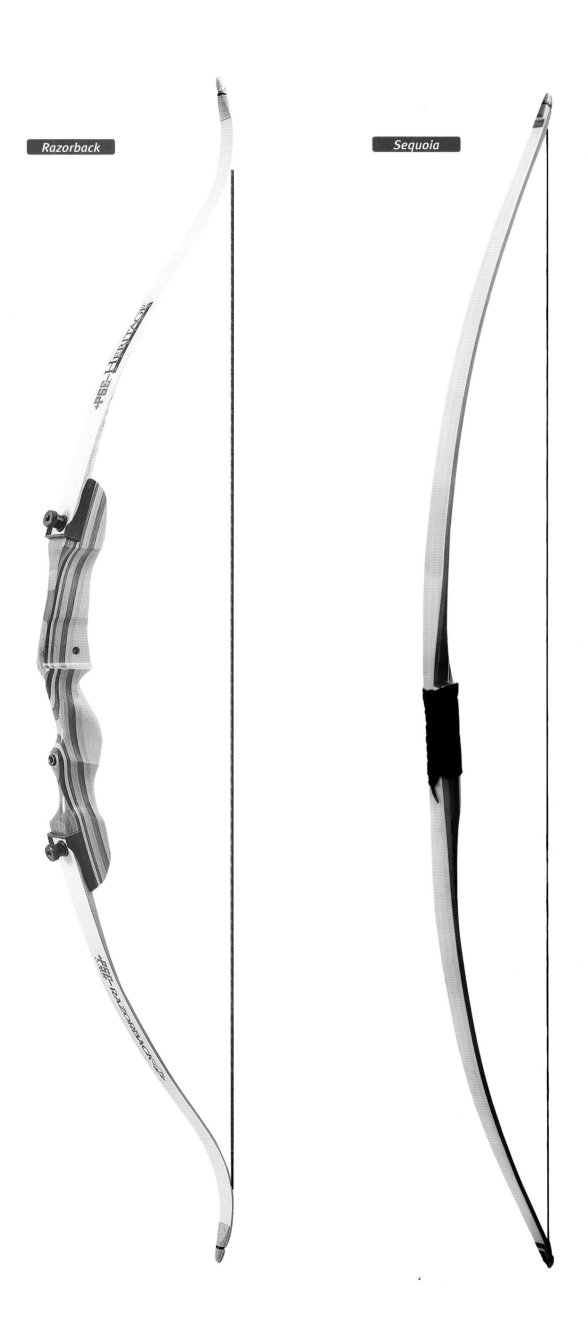

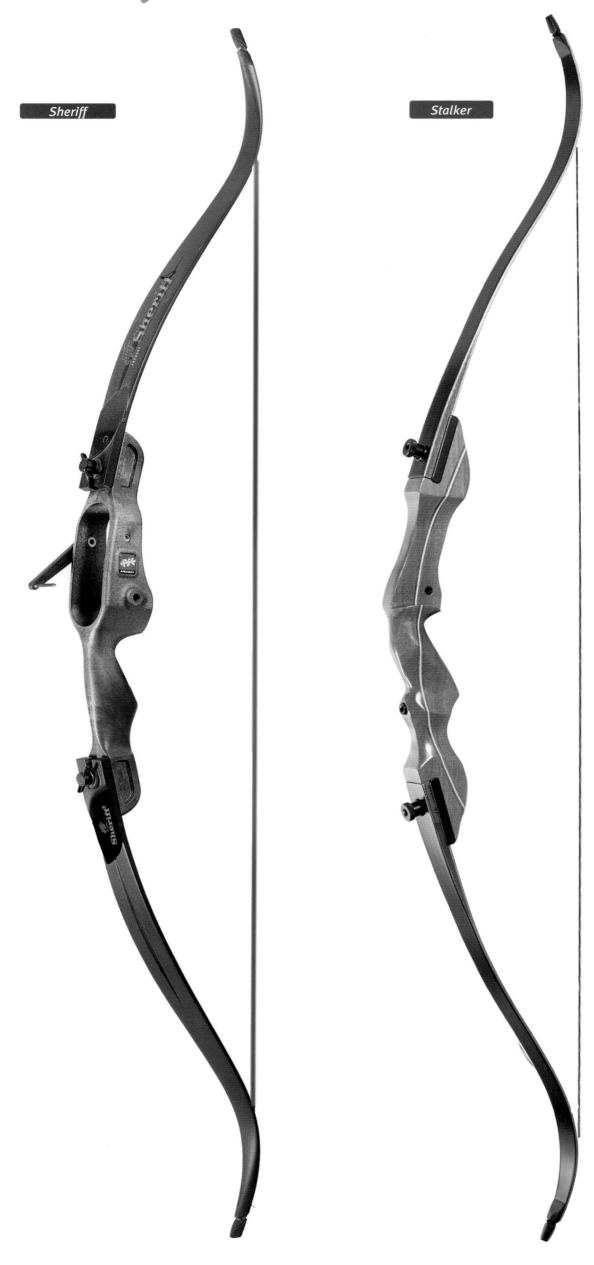

Sheriff

Stalker

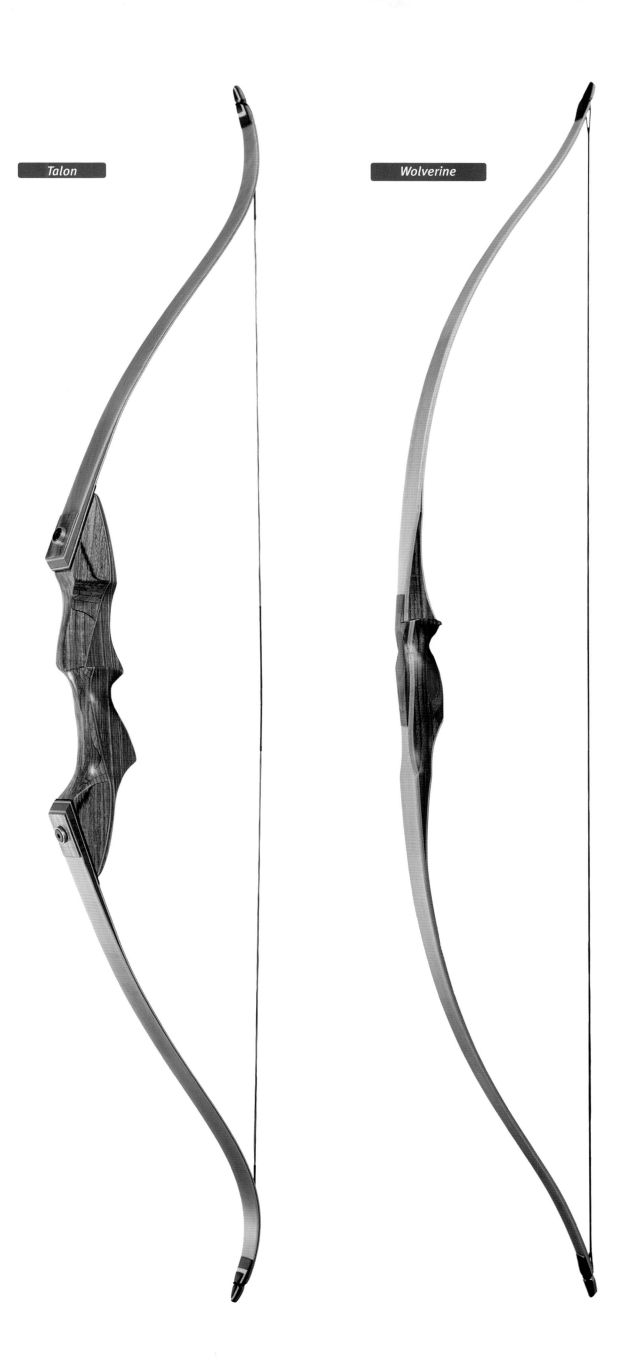

Talon

Wolverine

PSE Archery

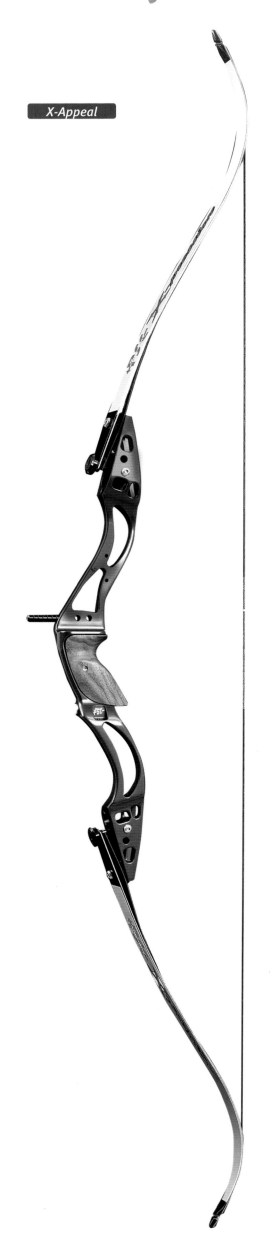

X-Appeal

X-Appeal Riser Red

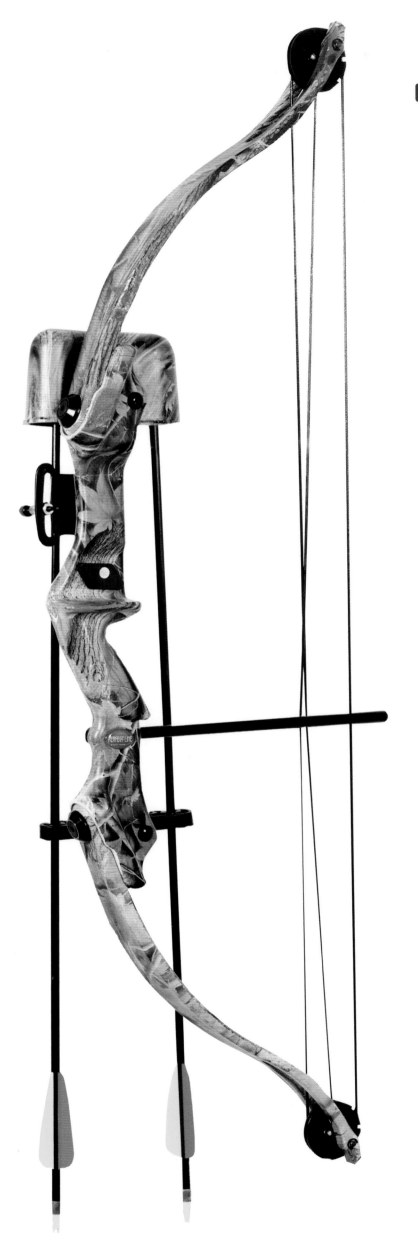

Ranger Compound

Bow Madness 3G

Brute X

Chaos FC Black/Camo

Deer Hunter

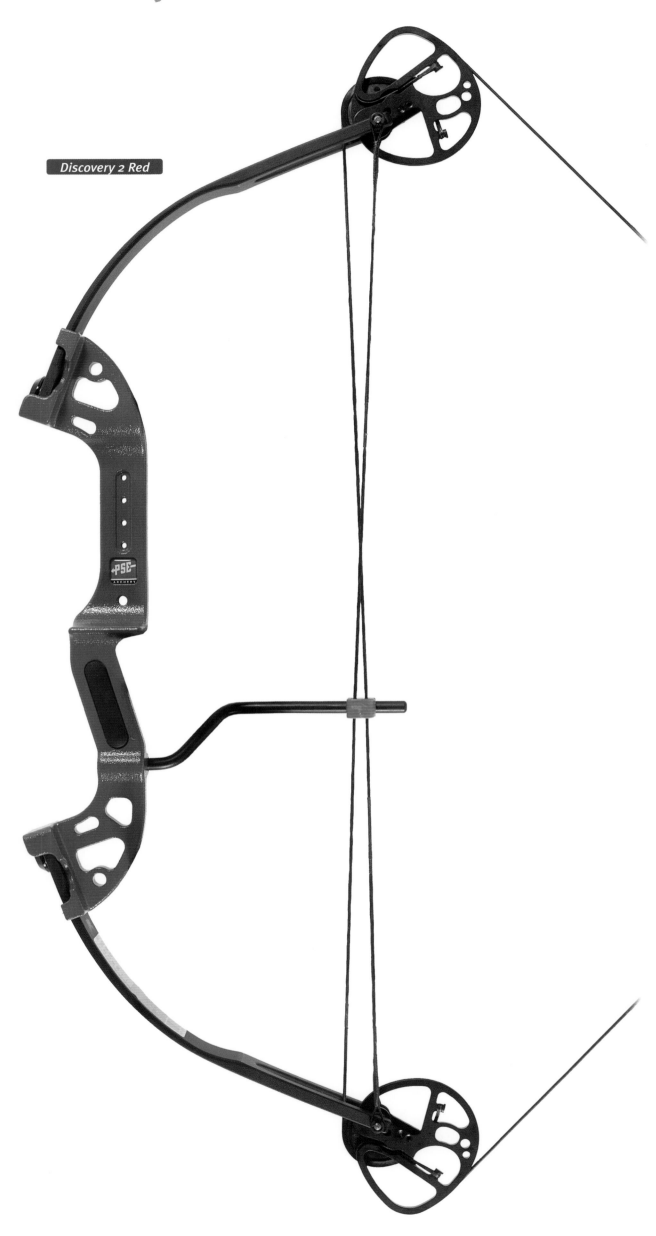

Discovery 2 Red

Mini Burner

Rally Bare Black

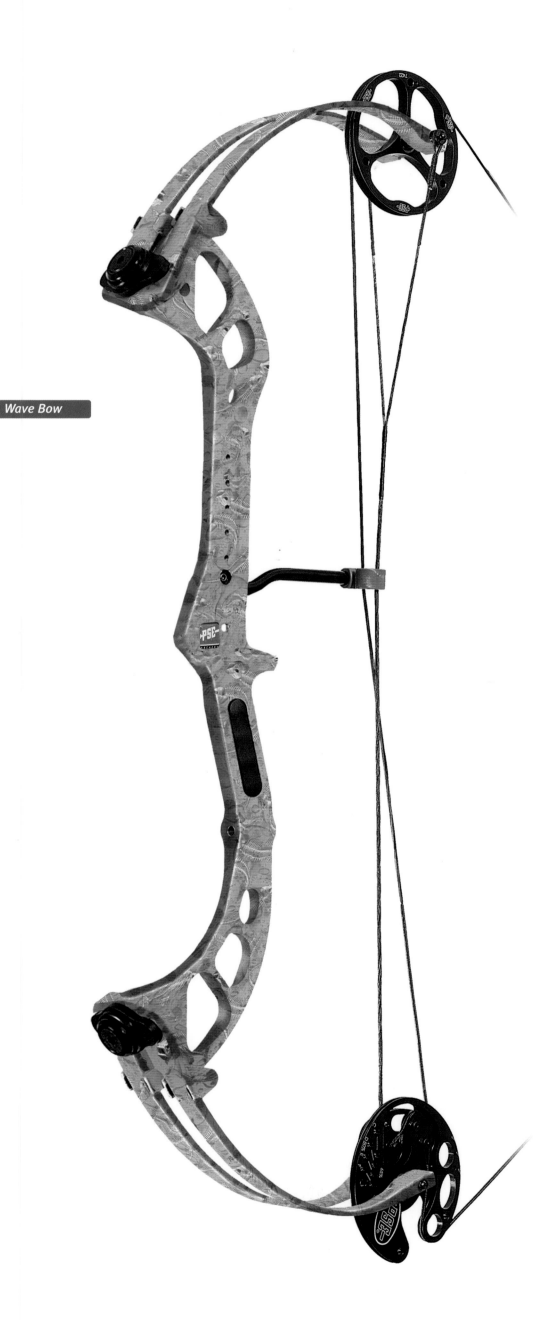

Wave Bow

Stinger 3G

Bow Madness XL Black

Rally

Bow Madness XS

X-Force Omen Pro

TAC 15

TAC 15i Combo

Quest Bowhunting

In 1966, Louis "Leo" Grace, Sr., started Grace Engineering in Memphis, Michigan. Twenty years later, Louis "Lou" Grace, Jr., assumed the leadership of the company. He further grew the business, focusing on precision manufacturing in the medical, hydraulic, and automotive industries as well as credit card embossing. With the help of his sons, Matt and Nate, Lou Grace founded G5 Outdoors in 2000 to market an all-steel broadhead. In 2001, the Montec, an all-steel three-bladed broadhead, was introduced. It was unique for its time and remains one of the company's top-selling broadheads.

In 2009, Quest Bowhunting entered the archery industry with the mission to bring to market a bow built with the highest level of craftmanship and quality, but at a reasonable price. The guiding principle of Quest is a sentiment stated by Leo Grace: "You're only as good as you can measure."

Quest bows are built to hunt. They feature ultra-smooth draw cycles, solid back walls, quiet shots, and accuracy. Five styles are available: Primal, Rev, Torrent, Rogue, and Torch. Quest bows have a DuraFuse finish, the company's patented process done with sublimation instead of water transfer. The process adds enormous durability (i.e., resistance to harsh weather and friction) and shelf appeal to the bow. Other technological innovations that Quest incorporates into its products are the Primal I-Glide Flex and forged risers.

Primal GFade Realtree

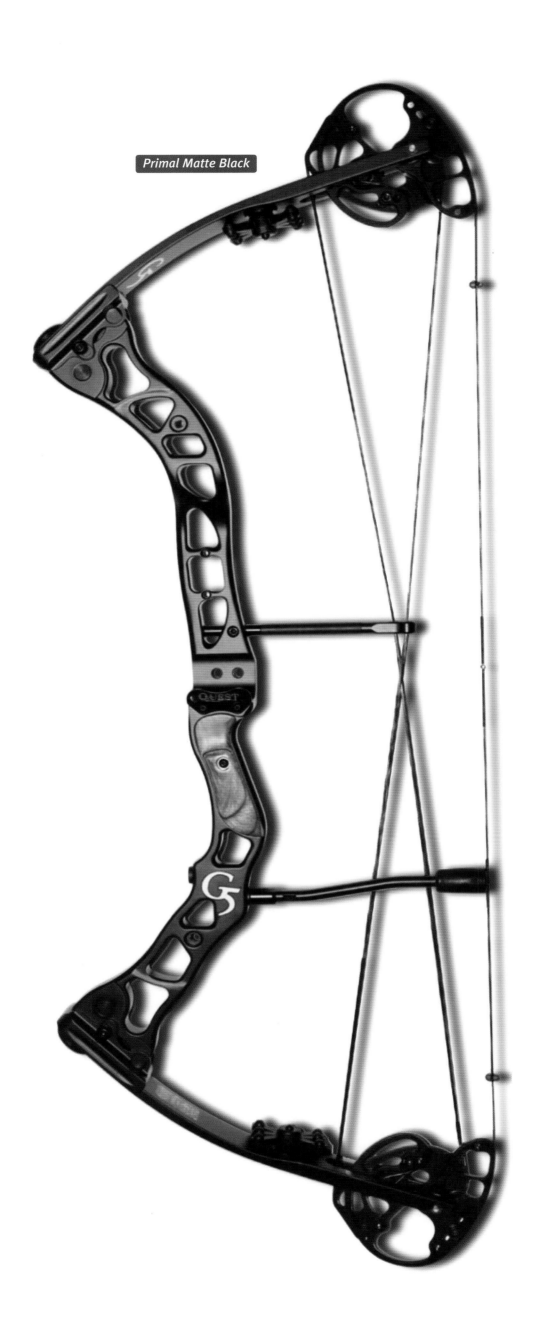

Primal Matte Black

Quest Bowhunting

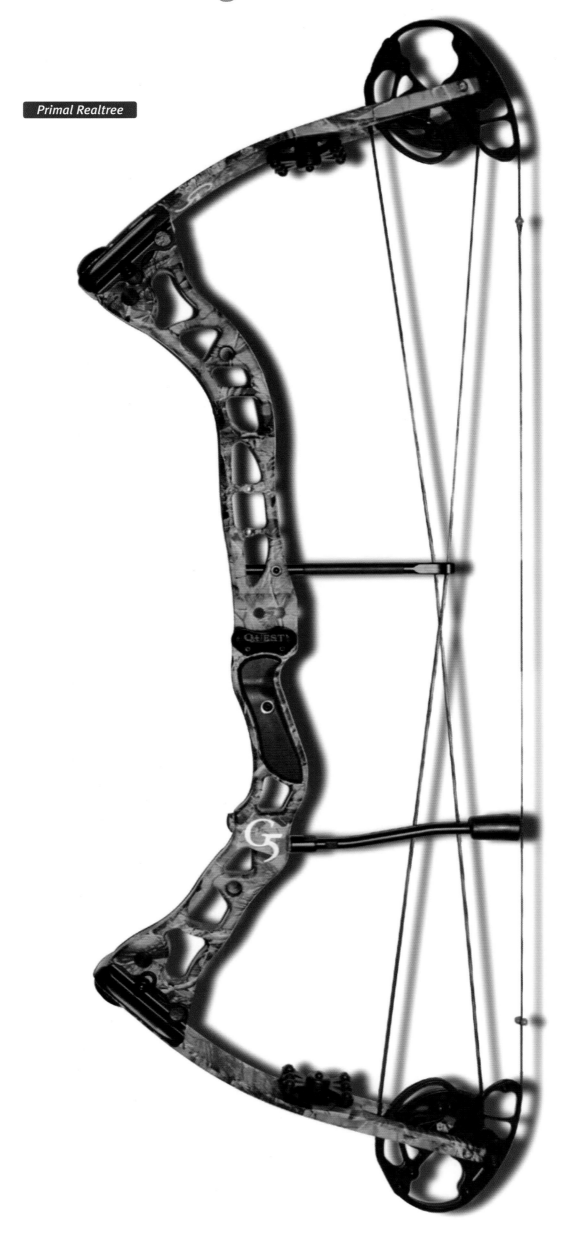

Quest Bowhunting

REV Realtree

Quest Bowhunting

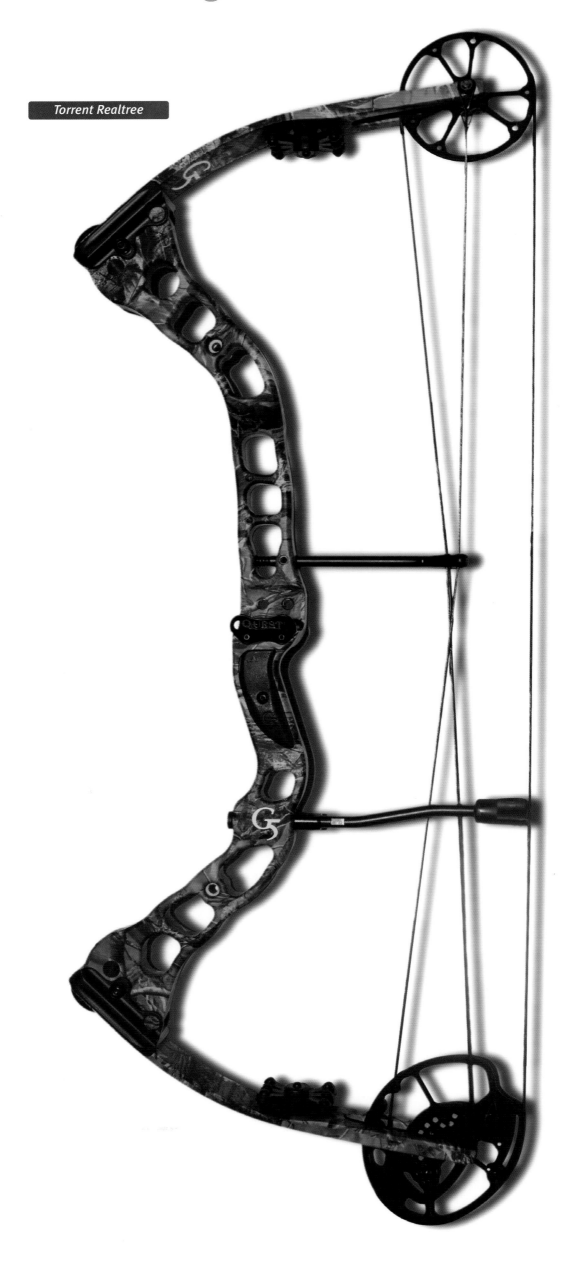

Torrent GFade Realtree

Rogue Realtree

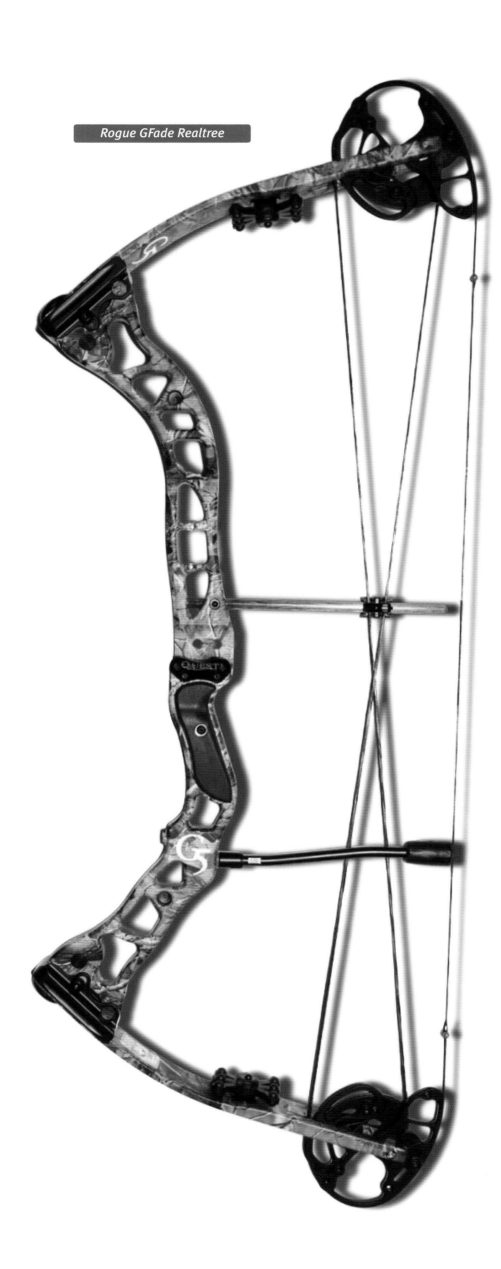

Rogue GFade Realtree

Torch GFade Realtree

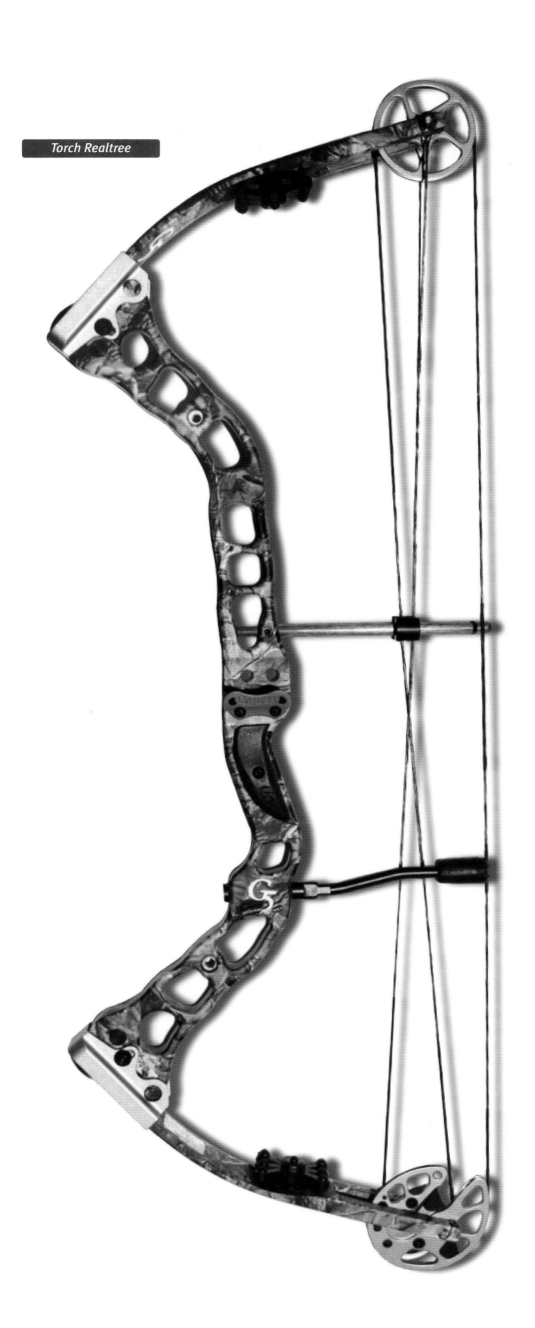

Torch Realtree

Quest Bowhunting

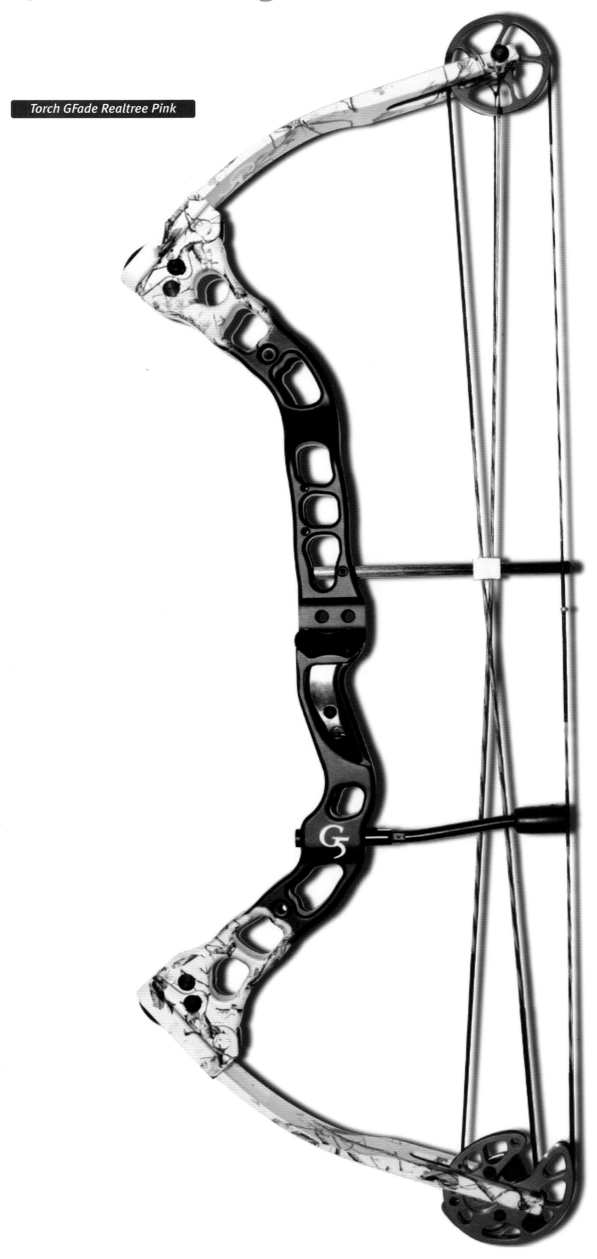

Torch GFade Realtree Pink

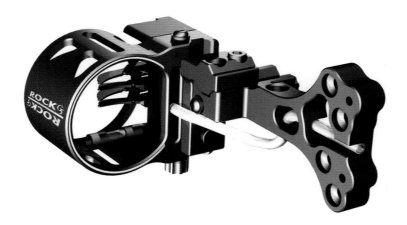

Quest Bowhunting

Five-Arrow Quiver
Camo

Five-Arrow Quiver

Sims 4.5-inch S-Coil
Stabilizer

**5-Pin Cobra Sight
with Light**

**Cobra Full-
Containment Rest**

**Axion
Stabilizer**

Winchester Archery

The Winchester name is nearly synonymous with shooting equipment, and has been for the last 140 years since the company's founding in 1866. Because bowhunting is a sport enjoyed by millions in the U.S. and around the world, it was a natural move for Winchester, the established firearms manufacturer, to make. The added challenges of archery make Winchester's reputation as a manufacturer of dependable outdoor hunting equipment a natural extension for the company.

Winchester Archery's stated mission is not only to produce high-quality, innovative archery equipment, but also to grow the bowhunting community, which the company refers to as Winchester Territory, so that avid outdoor huntsmen who appreciate the fine art and tradition of hunting can share experiences and "enjoy the ride" together!

All of the Winchester Archery products are designed, tested, and made in America. The company's crossbows are offered in eight styles: Lightning, Quicksilver 34, Quicksilver 31, Minx, Vaquero, Tracker, Thunderbolt, and Destiny. The crossbows are available in three styles: Stallion (350+ FPS), Blaze (330+ FPS), and Bronco (315+ FPS).

Winchester Archery is proud of technology's contribution to its products. The company's two-track technology for AST cam and ARC cams is patent pending. The same track of the cam performs both the cable take-up and cable let-out functions. The cam-to-cam rigging enhances accuracy and makes tuning the bow with a wide range of arrows a simple task. The AST cam is on the Quicksilver 31 and 34 crossbows, and the ARC cam is on the Vaquero and Tracker crossbows. Other technology features include, but are not limited to, directional venting in the risers; a choice of three different grip styles; stainless steel hardware; and speedsters that, as the name implies, help increase bow speed by increasing string momentum during the shot.

Check out Facebook, LinkedIn, YouTube, and Twitter for more information and news on Winchester Archery.

Lightning

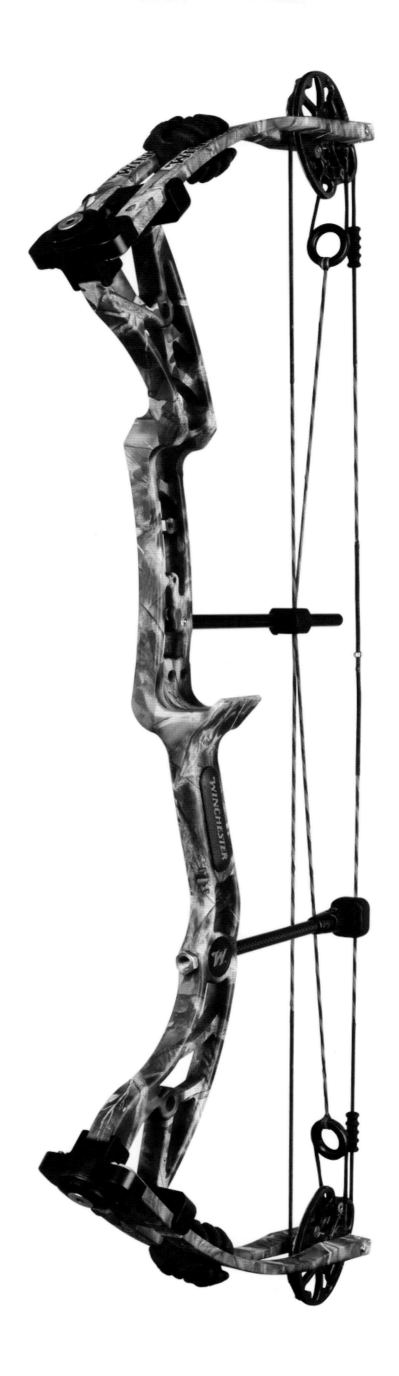

Winchester Archery

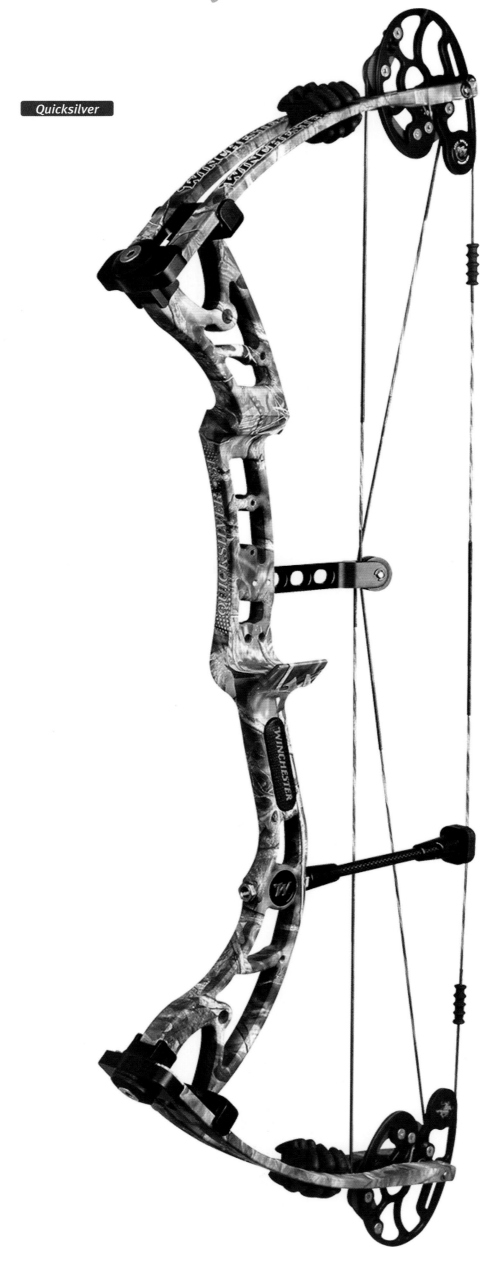

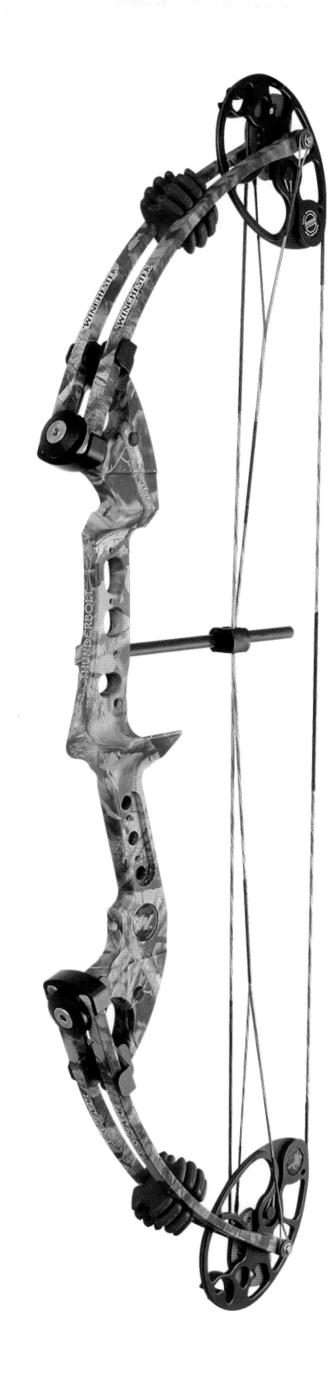

Thunderbolt

Winchester Archery

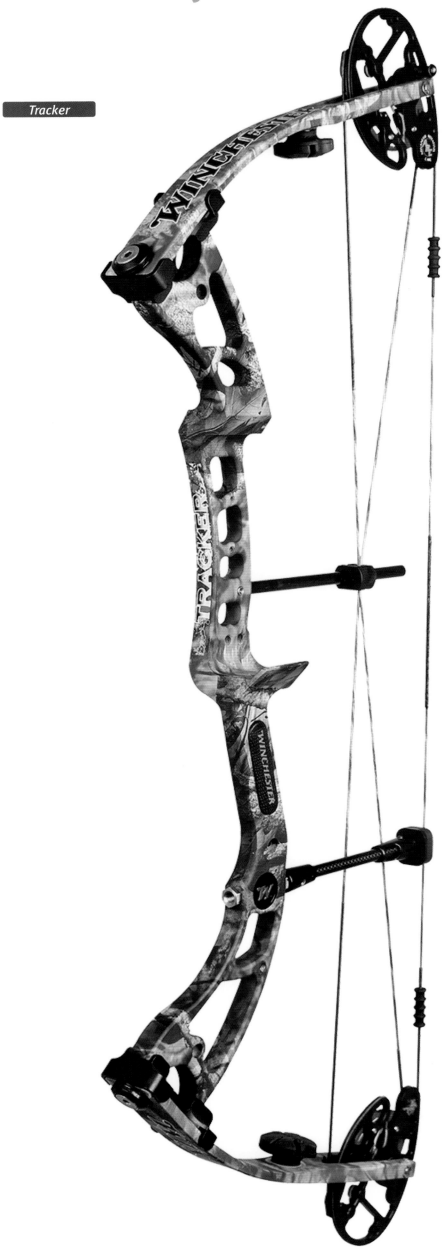

Winchester Archery

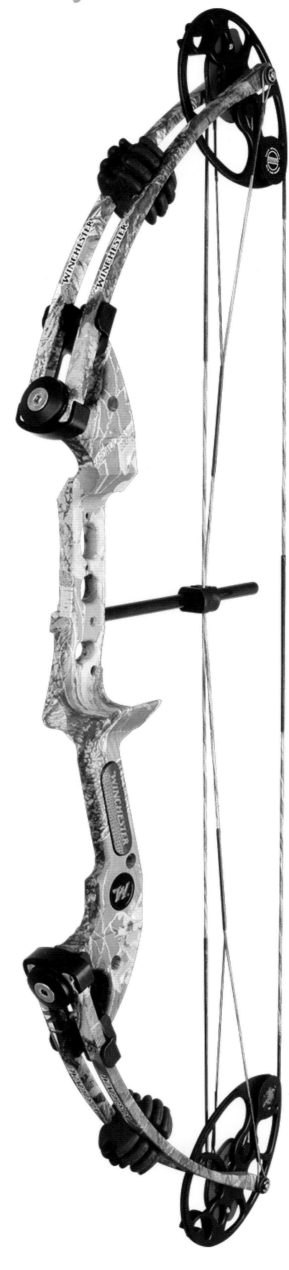

Maverick

Winchester Archery

Mustang

Stallion

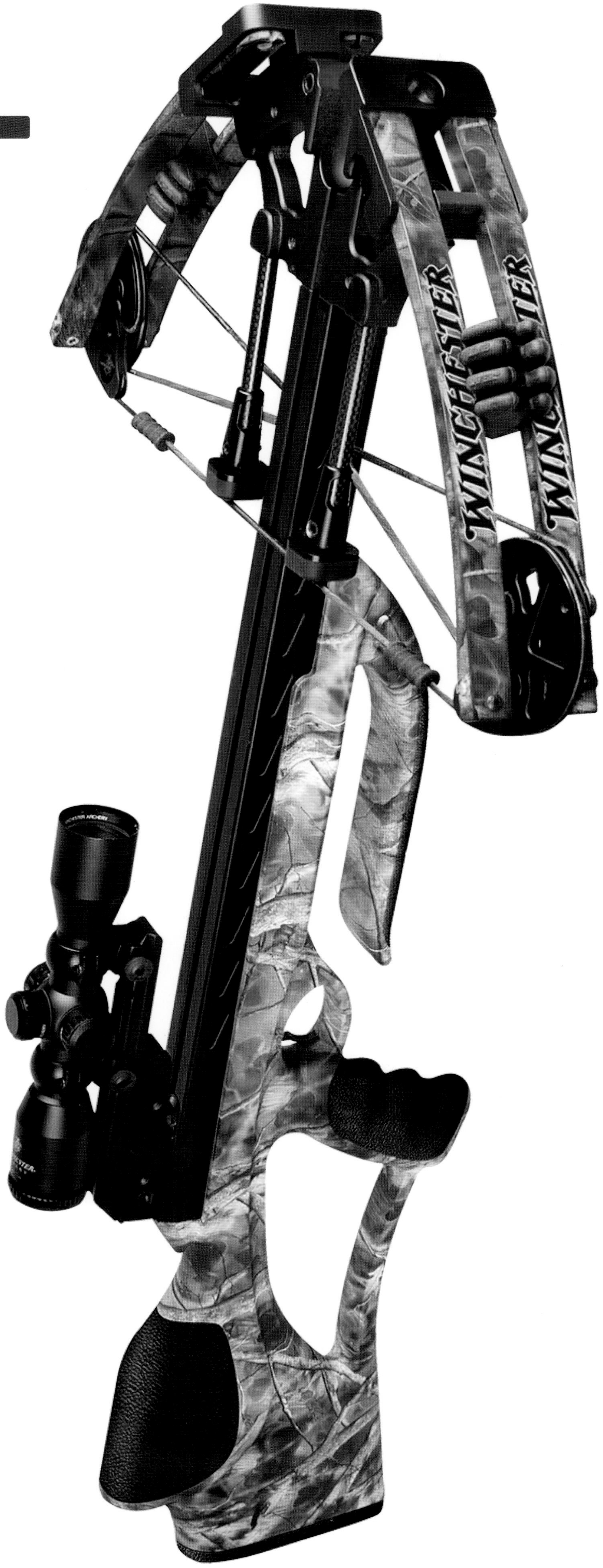

Index

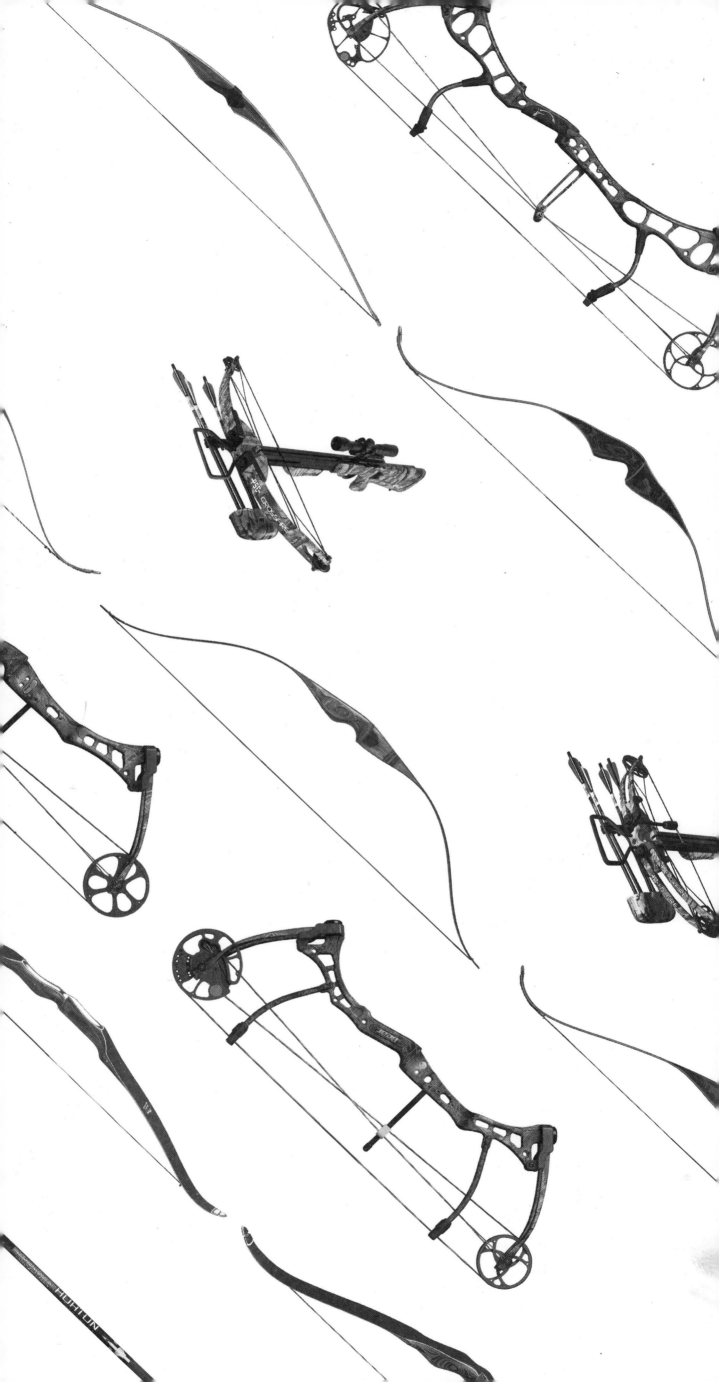

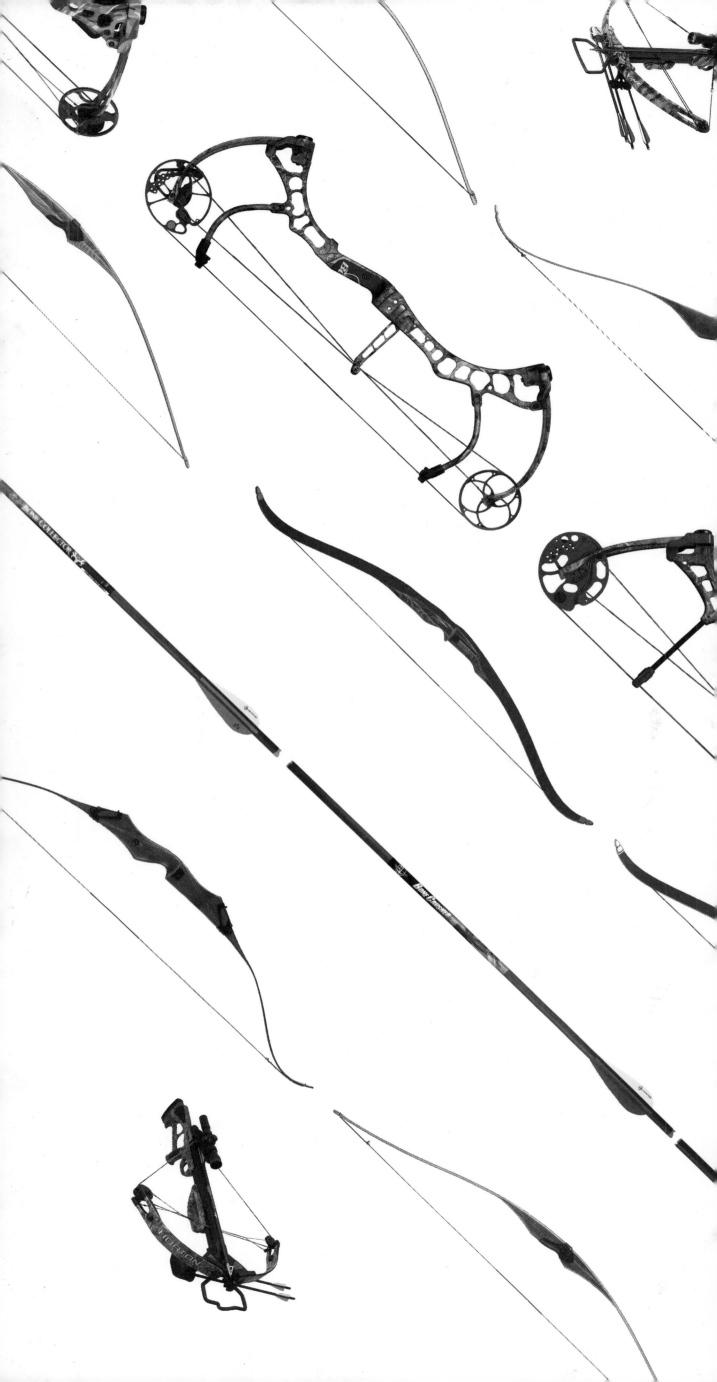